The Essex Coast

Photos, Drawings, Paintings & Digital Art by

Douglas Carpenter

ACKNOWLEDGMENTS

Many thanks to Jan Rodwell for advice and proof reading of my book and with whose help the book now makes much more sense.

Charles Grigg Tait 1915–1995 for inspiration and support to myself and others. Charlie a great art teacher, artist and author who lived in Maldon, Essex.

The Comprehensive Gazetteer of England and Wales, 1894

Essex Wildlife Trust for much information and interesting places to visit **http://www.essexwt.org.uk/**

Essex Walks - A informative free website listing rural walks in the Essex countryside **http://www.essexwalks.com**

Essex Birdwatching Society - the county bird society for Essex who collate data on the status of birds within Essex **http://www.ebws.org.uk/**

Sailing Tours Part 1 - The Thames to Aldborough by Frank Cowper

DEDICATION

To Brenda Carpenter without who's help the project would not be possible. Plus, the friends who have spurred on my enthusiasm to complete this project.

About The Essex Coast

A 350 miles exploratory Coastal Journey

The Essex Coast: a fascinating tour of Maritime Heritage.

The beautiful Essex countryside and its extensive coastline, with meandering rivers, canal and streams is a great county for boating, fishing or bracing coastal walks with splendid views. You can experience superb fresh seafood in rustic family run dining places such as The Sheds on Mersea Island, serving delicious local oysters, whilst watching the boats bobbing up and down on the River Colne. Then there's the vast salt marshes and shimmering mudflats that make up so much of the Essex coastline which were once the haunt of smugglers and oyster fishermen. Get a feeling of the old maritime Essex by taking a trip on the "Reminder" a Thames Sailing Barges often moored at Maldon. Alternatively, stop by the coastal town of Burnham-on-Crouch, referred to as "The Cowes of the East", with its famous yacht clubs.

Move on to Brightlingsea that comes alive with yachts and historic boats, competing during the summer boating season. The town is one of six Cinque Ports of England, but the only one situated on the East Coast.

The main islands of Essex are Horsey near Walton-on-the-Naze, Mersea at the mouth of Blackwater river, Wallasea which is bounded to the north by the River Crouch, to the south east by the River Roach. Foulness is the largest of the Essex islands and the fourth largest island off the coast of England is situated at the mouth of the Crouch River and is a vast and solitary expanse of isolated marshland. The most populated island being Canvey in the Thames Estuary.

The seaboard is low, flat, and partly marshy, has suffered much devastation by encroachments of the sea, with exception to some extent at Harwich and Southend. More vulnerable areas are now protected from further erosion by an extensive program of seawall defences put in place after 31st January 1953, when a great storm surge swept down the east coast of England and overcame the too flimsy sea defences, leaving 307 people drowned or dead from exposure, 120 of them from Essex. The worst hit communities in the county were Canvey Island, where 58 died, and Jaywick, where 36 people were killed.

The sometime Bleak Essex Coast is full of Drama

This Maritime Essex tour starts at the north boundary along the River Stour, it glides past Harwich at the mouth of the North Sea, heads south along the coast and finishes down river past Southend-on-Sea on the River Thames estuary. This part of the Thames coast promenades into the Greater London area, much of which was originally mapped as Essex.

Delightful visits on this tour include Walton-on-the-Naze, an early Victorian seaside resort, where you can stroll along the second longest pleasure pier in the country, or walk the staggering, ever changing Naze at Walton. Visit the Tower for a cup of tea with a most splendid view over the North Sea, if you can't manage the steps try the other nearby cafe with friendly staff and good refreshments or snacks to keep up your energy.

A £1.2m coastal erosion project to help preserve an area of the crumbling Walton Naze coastline has been completed. Around 16,000 tons of granite rock has been shipped in to build the walkway, which also includes a viewing platform overlooking the cliffs.

Walton-on-the-Naze lies on a narrow strip of land, approached by a long winding creek on the north which has its opening in Hamford Water. To the north-east of the old village of Walton the land rises to a kind of head land, and forms the promontory called the Naze. In Hamford Water are the little islands of Horsea and Holmes, and all this part of Essex bristles with Danish names.

Walton on the Naze Tower and Eroding Cliff

For something different try the quiet seaside town of Frinton-on-Sea, famed for its Art Deco homes and uncluttered seafront, which means no candy floss or sticks of rock. Indeed, the first pub and fish and chip shop only opened a few years ago. Flat firm sandy beaches between a series of ageing weathered timber groynes make this beach a place to relax and enjoy a swim or a picnic. Frinton-on-Sea beach is backed by sloping, crumbling cliffs. A quiet family resort to stroll along the beautiful seafront and take in the vistas of the North Sea with its multitude of wind turbines that seem to travel along the coast with you.

Dovercourt, facing the sea, is half-a-mile from Harwich on the wide estuary of the Orwell and Stour. Harwich has not much accommodation for visitors, but it is nearly always busy with shipping. The historic town, with an un-English look about it, influences from many years of immigration; there is a pleasant view across the estuary. Harwich is the terminus of the Great Eastern Railway, whose car-ferries run daily to and from the Continent terminating at the quay, Parkeston.

The anchorage and shelter at Harwich are so good that it is an important yachting centre. The estuary of the Stour bounds the rest of the Essex coast, and the tide is felt beyond Manningtree, which was a little junction on the Great Eastern Railway.

Find pretty villages which often have unique village signs, with typical Essex churches here and there the roof may have wooden tiles, sailing Centre's scattered with busy boat yards and great eccentric characters of the boating world, glorious steam boats or maybe the splendid fishing or oyster smacks which appear to be more sail than hulls. You may chance on the last skeletal remains of decaying boats, just about holding their ribs above water at low tide, preserved by the Essex mud - used to make the famed red brick for London, the Essex clay dug out at low tide and carried to the capital by the magnificent Thames Sailing Barges with their great red sails; often still seen in full sail around the coast.

This County was once infamously described by the High Tory James Wentworth Day as 'the dustbin of London'. Now the beauty of the Essex countryside and the extensive winding coastline, which takes in some of the most atmospheric estuaries and rivers to be found anywhere in the British Isles is now considered a prime location for residential and retirement home or the week-end "Caravanner" both static or touring.

In contrast Essex has the hustle and bustle from the docks and markets of the Thames Estuary. The climate that transform and often dramatically alters our coastline, as we cope with new ways of defense against rising sea levels. It tells us how tiny settlements grew into big holiday resorts and the way other villages have remained as charming small communities for centuries.

There are nineteen islands around the Essex coast a clusters north of Walton on the Naze others at the mouth of the Blackwater and Crouch and less known islands like Potton, New England and Ray dotted around the coast.

Rivers of Essex

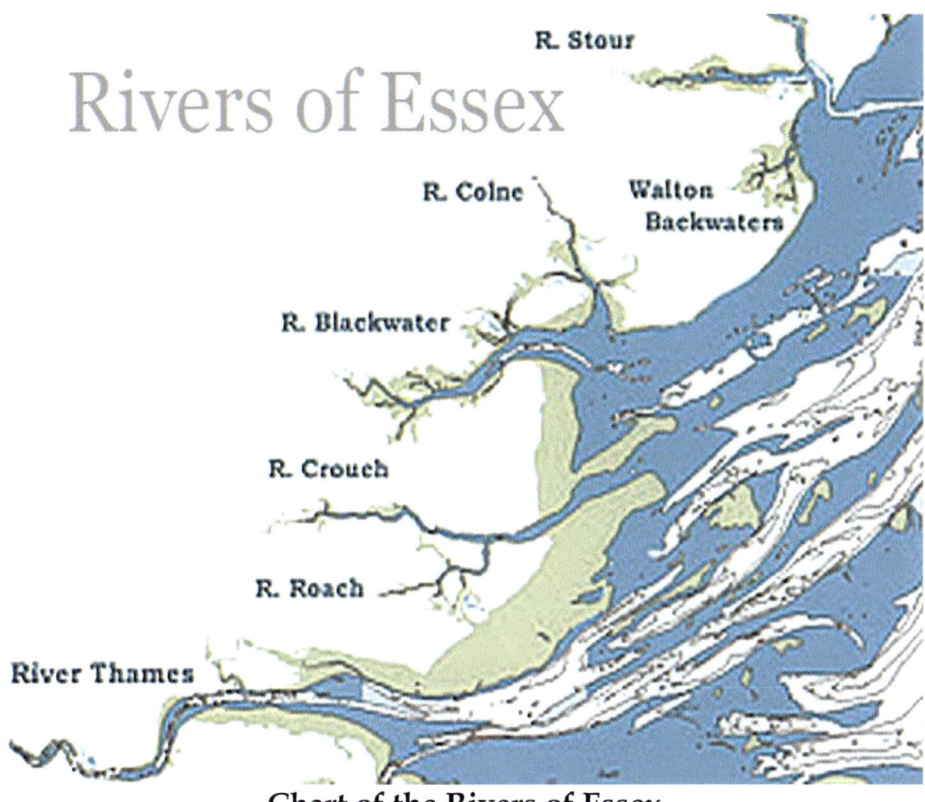

Chart of the Rivers of Essex

The main rivers of Essex, besides the Stour on the north of the county and the Thames to the south boundaries, are the Colne, the Blackwater, the Chelmer, the Crouch, the Roach, the Roding, the Ingerburn, and the Brain.

Essex is a county full of life and culture, inspiring and promoting local artists, writers, musicians and others who have fallen under the spell of the big skies with ramshackle hideaways and byways of its bohemian and radical history. Its coast is so irregular and broken that the exact length of it cannot easily be ascertained. From its most northerly port at historic Harwich on the estuary with the River Stour, the shoreline takes its winding journey with a variety of watery inlets, to the southern tip of Essex at Southend-on-Sea on the mouth of the River Thames. We finish at the Thames Flood Barrier where Essex use to be - but now merges with the capitol City of London.

A glance at the map of England will show that the insular features of Essex are quite different from those of any other county. Essex is the only county that has so many islands, large and small, quite close to its shores, and it will be well to consider them according to the river mouths in which they are situated. Canvey is in the Thames; an archipelago consisting of Foulness, Wallasea, Potton, Havengore, and New England are at the estuary of the Crouch; Northey and Osea are in the Blackwater; Mersea is at the estuary of the Colne; and Horsea, Holmes, Pewit, and many smaller islands are in Hamford Water, to the south of the estuary of the Stour. Many of these islands have certain characteristics in common. With the exception of Mersea, which is a little hilly, they are very low and marshy, and embankments have been constructed to prevent inundations. Most of them can be reached on foot at low water, and in most cases the surrounding sea is very shallow.

Shipping off the Essex Coast 1859

All round the Essex coasts it has been found necessary to build sea-walls; or to construct groynes for the protection of the land. In many respects the county presents a Dutch-like appearance, and the district behind Clacton is known as "Holland." Much has recently been improved from Clacton to Holland on Sea, with a £32-million-pound beach.

Kingfisher fishing an Essex River

'The Swatchways' a stretch of coast from Suffolk to South Essex of the East Coast known to the sailors of olden days. The definition of a coastal sea area made up of the rivers and creeks that abound between Foulness Island and the River Crouch to the southward and Aldeburgh to the north, embracing the Crouch, Roach, Blackwater, Colne, Mersea Quarters, the Stour, Orwell, Ore and the Alde, of which sailors could travel to the end of their high-tide navigability. Along the way are many muddy bays and creeks to explore and anchor in peace and tranquility, plus many a place to stop for a run ashore - or, nowadays, to rest in a marina that seems to nestle into the marshes thereabouts. Tidal, but that's what opens up the upper reaches and provides a good purpose to get there or back again. Muddy at low tide but with a good spattering of sandy beaches. Birds and seals abound to be viewed. Fish to be caught to enjoy with that evenings cocktails, or launch the dingie and head for the light glow of a friendly pub ashore. The Swatchways are not a secret. They are accessible, beautiful, still there to be shared and enjoyed by those with the appropriate vessels.

The book is illustrated with pictures, drawings and photographs some as digital art, as well as the narrative content which includes quite a few little-known facts and stories. It tells of the solitude of several of the most remote coastal regions of England and of the huge selection of wildlife to be discovered there. The eBook includes list of Essex Coastal nature reserve, wildlife Centre's and groups; plus, a list of the Essex Hundreds.

Essex Beach Huts on a Sunny Winters Day

2. Harwich

Harwich was constructed as a trading port by the Earls of Norfolk in the 13th Century. The export of cloth from local weavers was one source of the town's mediaeval prosperity. When the fortunes of the declining cloth industry were revived in the 16th century by Flemish weavers escaping persecution in the Low Countries, it was no doubt through the port of Harwich that many of them arrived in the area.

Harwich is an ancient seaport and market-town, created a municipal borough by Edward II in 1318. The place has developed considerably in modern times, mainly through the action of the Great Eastern Railway Company, in adopting it as a convenient point for their traffic between England and the Continent. The parish church of St. Nicholas for a long time merely a chapel-of-ease to the mother church at Dovercourt, was rebuilt of white brick, on a larger scale, in 1821, at a cost of about £20,000. The reconstruction included a new vestry, which is a miniature copy of the old church, some of whose contents are preserved in the present fabric, and, in fact, constitute its chief interest. Among these the octagonal font of Purbeck marble remains, with numerous mural tablets and monuments. There is a ring of eight bells, cast by T. Mears for the reconstructed church in 1821.

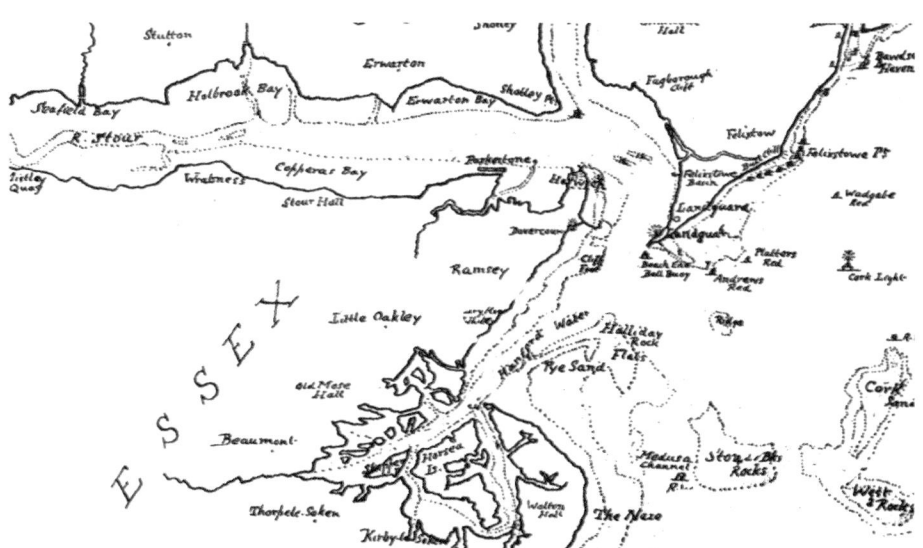

Harwich Hanford Water and The River Stour

Harwich Hanford Water and The River Stour with its continental ferries docking in the estuary at Parkeston quay, Harwich retains its unique character as a seafaring town which adds to the interesting historical flavour for the international traveler.

Its position on the estuaries of the Stour and Orwell rivers and its usefulness to mariners as the only safe anchorage between the Thames and the Humber led to a long period of maritime utilization, both civil and military. The town became a naval base in 1657 and was heavily fortified, with Harwich Redoubt, Beacon Hill Battery, and Bath Side Battery.

Harwich today is adjacent with Dovercourt and along with Parkeston, are often referred to jointly as Harwich. The town's name means "military settlement," from an Old English word here-wic. The town received its charter in 1238, although there is evidence of earlier settlement, there is a record of a chapel in 1177, and some indications of a possible Roman presence.

A Royal Navy Dockyard was established at Harwich in 1652. It was ideally positioned for preparation of the fleet in the Anglo-Dutch Wars of the seventeenth century. Thereafter its importance waned; the dockyard is generally said to have closed in 1713, but it continued to operate as a small storage and refitting base until 1829.

Harwich is home to Harwich & Parkeston F.C, Harwich and Dovercourt RFC, Harwich & Dovercourt Sailing Club, Harwich, Harwich & Dovercourt Rugby Union Football Club, Harwich & Dovercourt Cricket Club and Harwich Runners who with support from Harwich Swimming Club host the annual Harwich Triathlons run along the promenade and into the stunning local countryside.

Harbour at Harwich Ha'penny Pier and Quay

Built around 1854 as a ticket office for the steam package ships going as far as Margate or later the Continent. Now a very characterful tourist office with a little tea room opposite the pier office where you can sit and watch the marine activities round about you with a pleasant cuppa and cake in hand.

The Corporation Pier opened on 2nd July 1853 it was known officially throughout the 20th century as "Halfpenny Pier" because of the halfpenny toll charged, the pier extended in the north westerly direction for some 243 feet. Approximately half way along was a transverse easterly arm 213 feet long, 22 feet wide.

Because the Corporation was not able to repay its loans, the Great Eastern Railway slowly acquired a controlling interest in the pier, and the pier eventually became GER property in 1872. Despite the fact that deserted by the main continental ships after 1865, the Ha'penny Pier continued to be used by the railway's pleasure excursion vessels. The pier is now used to dock pleasure and other historical boats.

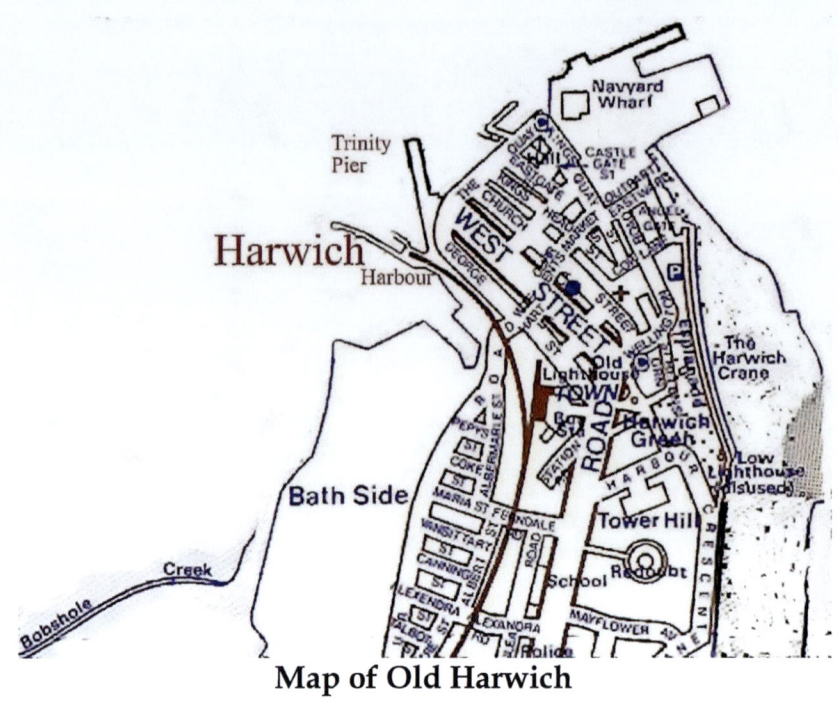

Map of Old Harwich

Harwich grew rapidly and in 1318 it was given a charter; by the later Middle Ages Harwich it was a busy little port. At that time England's main export was wool and bales were sent from Harwich. The main import was wine. Furthermore, in Harwich there were the craftsmen found such as carpenters, blacksmiths and stonemasons, useful to build by order of Henry VIII strong defences and forts. At that time Harwich was a busy fishing port with a population of about 800.

Harwich from the River Stour

Tug Boat displaying off Harwich during the Town Festival

In 1604 James I gave Harwich a new charter. As well as a weekly market Harwich was allowed 2 annual fairs. In those days' fairs were like markets but they were held only once a year. People came from all over Essex to attend the Harwich fair. In the 17th century Harwich continued to flourish and shipbuilding became a major industry in the town.

Treadwheel Crane

The Crane was used by the old navel yard from 1667 to 1927 operated by two men walking in the middle of the wheel, and is unique in the UK.

The Crane's wooden house, 26 feet 3 inches by 14 feet 10 inches, provides the frame, from which the 12 inches by 10 inches' thick jib projects 17 feet 10 inches. The crane was operated by a couple of men walking inside a pair of 16-foot diameter wooden tread wheels. The lifting chain wound around the axle to pass along the jib and over a wheel. There was no brake, and so a piece of wood was kept handy to jam the tread wheels to a halt. The cost of the crane was £392 to build and it served the docks for 260 years.

Samuel Pepys expanded the naval dockyard at Harwich in 1667 by command of the Duke of York, as part of plans to make Harwich a base for British ships in the sea war against the Dutch. He ordered the Treadwheel Crane as part of that expansion.

The dockyard closed in 1928, and in 1930 the crane was moved to Harwich Green, where it stands as a grand visitor attraction today which can only be viewed from the boundary.

Samuel Pepys by John Closterman

Christopher Jones House

Located in Kings Head Street; from 1620 Christopher Jones lived until he moved near to London. He was the master of the Mayflower Ship which took the first pilgrims to America. There is a plaque outside his house, placed there by the very diligent Harwich Society.

The Mayflower Project nearby is an enterprise based in the Mayflower ship's original home port of Harwich, Essex. The goal is to recreate a working replica of the Pilgrim Fathers' vessel, and to re-establish Harwich as a maritime centre and in addition, provide a centre of learning old skills for future generations, achieved by building a £2.5m replica of the ship which sailed to America in 1620.

This, it is hoped, will enhance Harwich as a maritime hub, reinvigorating the traditional boat building skills providing employment and educational opportunities throughout the surrounding areas.

The Mayflower was plausibly first launched in Harwich, in the county of Essex, she was designated as 'of Harwich' in the Port Books of 1609-11.

Harwich was the birthplace of Mayflower master Christopher Jones around 1570.

August 1609 records first note Christopher Jones as master and part owner of the Mayflower when his ship was chartered from London to Drontheim, Norway, and back to London. In a document of January 1611, Christopher Jones is described as being 'of Harwich', and his ship is called the "Mayflower of Harwich".

Harwich Lifeboat Museum

The Lifeboat Museum is a lovely old building that was the first lifeboat station to be used in 1821, and known for this reason as Number One Station.

The Harwich Lifeboat museum houses the old Clacton offshore lifeboat the "Valentine Wyndham-Quin", which is a 37 feet Oakley class of lifeboat. She was stationed at the Clacton Lifeboat station between 1968 -1984 and accomplished numerous honorable lifesaving services.

Harwich Lifeboat 17-03 Albert Brown

The Lifeboat was moved from Cromer to Harwich and the old Lifeboat house was re-opened and refurnished to accommodate her. The lifeboat museum now contains a large collection of miscellaneous and local lifeboat artefacts. Today there are two lifeboats stationed at Harwich; the off-shore Severn class lifeboat "Albert Brown" and the inshore Atlantic 75 lifeboat "Sure and Steadfast".

The Three Mast Schooner 'HMS Beckford'

High Lighthouse on the main road to Harwich

The High Lighthouse was sold for £75 (without usage restrictions) and was used as a residence. The High Lighthouse now contains a privately run Wireless Museum - note the lifebuoy in the foreground, a relic from Trinity House whose duty lies in the safety of sailors and shipping, using an impressive array of over 600 aids to navigation, ranging from lighthouses to a satellite navigation service. Trinity House which is opposite the docks, was granted a Royal Charter by Henry VIII in 1514.

Traditional rig sailing ships under 120 feet. Completed June 1955 as Seaward Motor Launch the HMS Beckford. She went into reserve on completion until refitted in 1964 and renamed HMS Dee for Mersey Royal Naval Reserve. Loaned to the Plessey Group for a period for radar trials in 1968 as Robert Clive, then reverted to HMS Dee. Replaced on the Mersey in 1981, she was sold and converted to sailing vessel and renamed HMS Beckford.

Harwich Redoubt Fort an anti-Napoleonic circular fort

The Redoubt a fortress built to fend off Napoleon around 1808, which was never used in anger. A super impressive 180ft (60m) diameter circular fort was built in 1808 to defend the port of Harwich against a Napoleonic invasion. It is the only such example open to the public. Eleven guns are placed on its battlements. Eighteen casements below would house 300 troops in siege conditions. Part of the fort now contains three small military museums. Battle re-enactments and other events are held during the summer months. The Redoubt is being restored by the Harwich Society.

Napoleonic Re-enactors at the Redoubt Fort

The Harbour at Harwich

Moored in the harbour is a colourful lightship, being use as a temporary Radio station the LV18 lightship built in 1957 was remotely controlled rather than manned. The ship was decommissioned in 1990 and became the pirate BBC Radio Essex station. After being restored by volunteers, it is now birthed at Harwich Quay as a tourist attraction and exhibition ship. Visitor opening hours are 11 to 5pm - March to October.

Harwich Quay late 1800s

Harwich with its fine Harbour, horses pulled rail trucks on Harwich quay with Customs House and Halfpenny Pier.

The Electric Palace Cinema, Harwich

The Electric Palace in Harwich, first opened its doors in 1911 is the oldest purpose-built cinemas to survive complete with its silent screen, original projection room and ornamental frontage still intact.

Other interesting features include an open plan entrance lobby with its red pay box, and a small stage plus dressing rooms although the latter are now unusable. There is also a former gas powered generator engine with a 7-foot fly wheel situated in the basement.

The cinema was built in 18 weeks at a cost of £1,500 and opened on Wednesday, November 29th, 1911, the first film being The Battle of Trafalgar and The Death of Nelson. The creator of the Palace was Charles Thurston, a travelling showman well known in East Anglia, and the architect was Harold Hooper, a dynamic young man of 26 years who demonstrated his creative flair with this his first significant building. The cinema closed in 1956 after 45 years, interrupted only by the 1953 floods and was listed as a building of sociological interest in September 1972 and is now a Grade II listed building. It re-opened in 1981 and now runs as a community cinema showing films every weekend.

The Electric Palace cinema runs as a club and the annual fee is FREE to members from 1st January 2015. A small amount will be collected with each admission ticket and handed to the Harwich Electric Palace Trust.

Membership can be arranged at the Box Office or by emailing boxoffice@electricpalace.com King's Quay Street, Harwich, CO12 3ER

The Electric Palace in Harwich

The Low Lighthouse now Harwich Maritime Museum

Harwich Maritime Museum located in the former Low Lighthouse which was built in 1818 as one of a pair of leading lights for the harbour entrance at Harbour Crescent. An active radio link to harbour control serves as a reminder of the lighthouse's time as a pilot signal station.

The small museum is full of nautical memorabilia from photographs, paintings, lighthouse bulbs and ships in bottles. There are displays on the Royal Navy, including uniform and badges, and local commercial shipping. A fantastic view of the shipping activity in the harbour is obtained from the top floor.

Adults £1 Children must be accompanied by an adult and are free of charge.

Opening Times; Friday, Saturday & Sunday; 11.00 to 3.00 Open from 1st May to 31st August (subject to change).

Cast Iron Lighthouses at Dovercourt

Built to replace the old brick built ones at Harwich, none of which are in use today. Called the Low and High lighthouses, you could steer a ship using the distance between the lighthouse. The replacement little and large cast iron lighthouses, sited one on the beach the other in the sea at Dovercourt, serve the same navigational purpose.

Dovercourt bay, which is about a mile from Dovercourt town and the Port of Harwich, a historic and admirable seaside resort of modest means, the sea and land views can be compared to that of the bay of Naples, on the left you have dramatic views of Felixstowe, Languard and Harwich forts, with a great variety of shipping entering the harbour, looking to the right is Walton on the Naze with its distinguished Naze Tower plainly visible.

Harwich International Sea Shanty Festival

A full weekend of Sea Songs and Shanties during the month of October in the historic seaport of old Harwich.

A mixture of free open air entertainment, concerts, music sessions, classic boats, pub sessions and sing-a-longs during the festival weekend. Events take place throughout the old town of Harwich at venues including the Ha'penny Pier, Harwich Town Sailing Club, The Redoubt Fort, The New Bell Inn, The Alma, The Hanover and The Stingray, Samuel Pepys Wine Bar, Crown Post Restaurant, The Harwich and Dovercourt Sailing Club and on board classic boats.

The Foot Ferry service to Shotley operates over the weekend, for an entirely different perspective of Harwich and enjoy the hospitality of the Shipwreck Inn, with entertainment from Festival Guests.

The Thames Sailing Barge "Victor" is running one and a half hour trips from the Ha'Penny Pier with on board entertainment from Festival Guests.

At the Redoubt are held Traditional Maritime Crafts, Workshops and Napoleonic displays.

Pirates on Harwich Green encampment with sword fighting, pistol shooting, skirmishes and cannons, plus costumed displays of 18th & 19th Century living.

Thames Sailing Barges, Reminder and Thistle

Parkeston

The Quay and the village was partially on an island called "Ray Island" and partially on mud flats of the River Stour. Ray Island was not in reality an island all the time, only at high tide. At low tide it was linked to the mainland by a stretch of marshland.

"Brilliance of the Seas" at Harwich International Cruise Terminal

Parkeston Quay is located on land originally called "Le Rey" a name given during the Saxon period. In the early nineteenth century Lewis Peake Garland had a dyke system constructed around the area of "Le Rey" or "The Ray" as it has become known. Ray Island stood there undisturbed for hundreds of years. It had changed ownership and its name a few times but otherwise was unchanged. Before this Ray island would have been encircled by water at high tide and by the estuary mud and marsh at low tide. The tide came in passed what is now Bathside Bay and flowed round the Island re-joining the main river where there is now an oil refinery.

The new quay was opened for business in 1883 and retained the name of Harwich but was called 'Stour Quay'. That was subsequently changed to Harwich (Parkeston) Quay, named after Charles H. Parkes, Chairman of the G.E.R. British and foreign travelers have been bewildered by the name ever since.

Manningtree, Mistley and The River Stour

Manningtree is England's smallest town at just over 19 hectares the town is best known to the outside traveller by the railway station on the main London to Norwich line, but the most familiar landmark to the local traveller is Mistley Towers.

A market-town of some importance on the south bank of the Stour, at the western extremity of its navigable portion. The town constitutes the parish of the same name, and includes parts of the adjacent parishes, Lawford and Mistley, from the latter of which it was formed.

Manningtree from offshore - Digital Art

Manningtree can offer the keen walker a host of pleasant walks many of which form part of the Essex Way. This walk is a long-distance path stretching right across the County of Essex from Epping in the south-west through Manningtree to the port of Harwich in the north-east. Following footpaths and ancient green lanes it covers a distance of 81 miles.

The River Stour born upon the borders of the adjoining county of Cambridge, and running an almost parallel course with the Colne. The river begins to act as the county boundary at Kedington. Passing a curve of the river, to the Essex town of Sudbury, the birthplace of the painter Gainsborough, and the point from whence the Stour becomes navigable. With smaller villages in close succession settled along its course, the Stour at Higham is joined by the River Bret, and the territory between Higham and the town of Manningtree is the countryside which inspired the great British artist John Constable who lived at Dedham. The artist was never tired of saying that the picturesque landscape of the Stour valley is what made him a painter.

The Mistley Towers

The towers are from the 18th century and made to complement the Georgian church of St Mary the Virgin at Mistley. One of only two churches designed by Robert Adam. The towers, in typical Adam classical style, stood at each end of the church, which is no longer in existence. The Ten Commandments written up on the inside wall of one tower.

In 1776 local landowner Richard Rigby commissioned Robert Adam to enhance the existing church, and turn it into a truly grand edifice. Rigby's father a wealthy gentleman by shrewd speculation by South Sea investments in the early 18th century. One of the things he did with that fortune was to build a new church in 1735, at the north end of Mistley village then known as Mistleythorn. Richard Rigby augmented his father's fortune when George III named him Paymaster General of the Armed Forces. Rigby had grandiose plans for Mistley, including making it into a fashionable spa. His father's plain brick church did not fit in with those plans, so he engaged the architect, a master of the neoclassical style, to design a new church.

St Mary's the Virgin Church, Mistley c1738

Mistley is a parish on the south bank of the navigable Stour, partly included in the town and parish of Manningtree. The church of St Mary & St Michael Church is at New Road, Mistley and replaces the Robert Adams church that was between and part of the Mistley Towers, erected in 1870-71 to supersede the old fabric, from which the most important monuments have been preserved. Otherwise the contents, though costly and in excellent taste, are of no antiquarian interest. The tower bears a tall spire (140 ft.), and contains a ring of six bells, one dated 1747, and five 1898, when they were dedicated on Lady Day in memory of Queen Victoria's Diamond Jubilee. If you cross the road, and walk with an eye to the grass, you will spot a rectangular piece of grass, greener than the rest, under it is said to be the grave of Matthew Hopkins the Witch Finder General of Essex.

Edme is a well-known malting company founded in the 1880s, with an array of tall imposing buildings at Mistley, (some are now residential flats) consisted of warehouses, a granary, a large malting office and new quays.

The first Mistley Quay was built around 1720 and about 1770, the quay was enlarged by Richard Rigby and became the Port of Mistley. Small-scale shipbuilding took place – the Reminder was the last steel hull Thames barge to be built here. There were also a number of smaller warships were built for the Royal Navy at Mistleythorn during the 18th century.

The Mistley Quay Workshops at Swan Basin serves freshly cooked breakfast, lunch, coffee and tea with panoramic views of the River Stour. Opposite is 'Cooper's Gallery' selling fantastic local arts and crafts. The Quay is again open to the public after a few sad years of being fenced off.

A Roman road leading from Mistley to the nearby provincial capital of Roman Britain at Camulodunum now Colchester, has led to the suggestion that there may have been a port in the vicinity of the modern village which served the town in the Roman period.

3. Walton-on-the-Naze

Walton on the Naze Beach

Walton-on-the-Naze is one of Britain's traditional seaside towns, the pier with its amusements and funfair is the third longest pier in Great Britain. This has the world's oldest operating amusement parks offering tenpin bowling, rides, bingo and refreshments throughout the year being mostly under cover, and holds frequent alfresco concerts.

Walton on the Naze Seafront looking towards the Pier

To the north of the town is a stretch of rapidly eroding cliffs and foreshore known as The Naze. The erosion has caused the cliff to retreat by one to two metres every year, threatening nearby land and buildings. The Naze is a 'site of special scientific interest', as it has fifty-five-million-year-old fossils being exposed from the crumbling cliffs, making it very valuable for scientific research. The fossiliferous clays and sands exposed by erosion are a type of London Clay or red crag formations, and provide evidence of prehistoric life and the conditions of millions of years ago.

The sea reaches the beach by longshore drift and erodes the cliff by weathering, hydraulic action and abrasion. The cliff is being eroded back and this means land and buildings will be lost. Maybe one day the tower itself will land up on the beach below with the concrete gun towers already there - if left to the eroding sea. The Naze Protection Society was formed to campaign for erosion controls and have had some success recently.

The parish was earlier known as Walton-le-Soken. The name 'Walton' is a common word meaning a 'farmstead or village of the Britons', while 'Soken' denotes the soke (an area of special jurisdiction) that included Thorpe, Kirby and Walton.

The old lifeboat station and the new coastguard building give a fascinating insight into the maritime history of Walton-on-the-Naze which is home to a busy coastguard and lifeboat station and has been so since 1880s. The records of lives and ships saved are engraved on plates surrounding the Lifeboat Station in the days of pirate radio in the 1960s, the Walton lifeboat was frequently in attendance to the pirate radio ships in distress of which the most famous are; Radio Caroline and Radio London, both were moored off the North Essex Coast. Walton Maritime Museum regularly holds special exhibitions such as "That's Entertainment", a display illustrating how the residents and the holidaymakers were entertained in Walton and Frinton in the first half of the twentieth century.

Frinton & Walton Heritage Trust maintains and operates the world's oldest surviving motor lifeboat. You can now book a trip on this boat which sails from Walton-on-the-Naze.

The old lifeboat Station Walton Maritime Museum

The museum housing a collection of Walton memorabilia in a restored old lifeboat house. The most significant object is the James Stevens No 14, the oldest surviving motor lifeboat in the world. The museum explores its own and other local lifeboats stories, together with fishing and boat building customs, coastal defence, and Walton as a seaside resort. The local coastal geology and erosion of the Naze displays are popular with schools. There are various annual changing exhibitions on maritime and other themes.

Admission Costs Adults £1, accompanied children under ten-year-old free. The museum is open every day from July from 1400 to 1600. (Subject to change.)

The new coastguard station lifeboat is moored near the end of the pier and is the only lifeboat in Britain to have a permanent mooring in the open sea. When necessary, the crew cycle the length in the pier after which they use a tiny launch to access the lifeboat.

The Thames branch in the Maritime & Coastguard Agency is the new coastguard station based at Walton, monitoring ship distress calls and coordinating search and rescue operations for the whole of East Anglia.

Walton and Frinton has celebrated over 120 years as a lifeboat station and its crews have been presented with 75 awards for gallantry. The lifeboat was one of 19 lifeboats that helped to evacuate the British Expeditionary Force from Dunkirk. Approximately 198,229 men along with 139,997 French and some Belgian troops, were evacuated from Dunkirk between 26 May and 4 June 1940; abandoning much of their equipment after disabling their vehicles and main weapons.

The Old Lifeboat House, East Terrace, Walton-on-the-Naze, Essex, CO14 8PY

Walton-on-the-Naze Pier

Walton's first pier was badly damaged by storms in the 1890s, before a replacement was built in 1895 by the Walton-on-the-Naze hotel and pier company, 500 ft longer (150 m) than the original. Several extensions have increased the pier's length to 2,600 ft (790 m), the third longest in the UK. When the new pier opened in 1895, an electric tramway was installed to take passengers from the steamers to the front of the pier. In 1945 fire damaged the pier, and the carriage was replaced by a diesel locomotive train. This was removed during the 1970s.

The covered pier is great for inclement weather housing fair rides and amusement arcades, and all the fun of the fair, or stroll to the end to see the new lifeboat. Although officially the third longest pier in the UK at over half a mile long, Walton Pier is by far the longest going out into the open sea which makes it ideal for sea fishing. The Tenpin Bowling on the pier is open every day from 10am.

John Weston Nature Reserve is situated towards the end of the Naze along the eroding public footpath that saunters through the cliff tops woods after passing by the Naze Tower or descend the steps and stroll along the beach to reach the reserve which is owned by the Essex Wildlife Trust.

Walton on the Naze Eroding Cliffs

Nesting birds consist of sedge, redshank, lapwing and reed warblers, the latter having colonized the reeds. Beyond the reserve is a 1.5-mile-long shingle beach, ending at Stone Point, which is a regular nesting home for small tern and other shorebirds. It's a crucial land stop for migrant birds of which there are rare example of the firecrest and barred warbler to name a few.

The reserve is named after the late John Weston, a well-known Essex naturalist who was warden of the reserve until his death in 1984. The reserve being so close to the shore, also attracts shore-loving insects, like emperor moth, cream-spot tiger moth and saltern ear moths. Join the path on the cliff top, bear left and stroll along the embankment, above and look down on pools and marshes at the edge of the Essex Wildlife Trust nature reserve. Where the path ends, bear left once more to continue along a pleasant grassy path above Cormorant Creek with the surrounding scenic marshland. The Naze Tower dominates the skyline for the left. The island of Hamford Water and the Tower are the location of Arthur Ransome's Swallow and Amazons book.

The Naze Defense Towers that use to be on top of the cliff

The Hanoverian tower, more commonly known as the Naze Tower, is situated at the start of the open area of the Naze. It was a navigational tower, constructed to assist ships on this otherwise fairly feature-less coast.

The Naze Tower museum explores the fascinating history of the Naze and provides information on the ecology and geology nature, the coastal erosion problem and the Crag Walk coastal scheme. A collection of fossils and artefacts found at the Naze are on display. Trinity House built the 86ft octagonal Naze Tower in 1721 to guide shipping to the busy port of Harwich. Originally housing a beacon, it is the predecessor of the reflective lighthouse that became commonplace in the 19th century.

The Naze Tower is a Grade II listed building of unique architectural and historic interest and is the only one of its type in existence. The building is in the top 5% of heritage buildings and the top twenty listed lighthouses in the country.

Over the years the Tower has had many uses, especially during times of war. More recently it lay derelict until it was extensively renovated and opened to the public for the first time ever in its history in 2004. The local family who own the Tower undertook the splendid restoration and still run the Tower today.

The place-name "Naze" derives from Old English næss "ness, promontory, headland". In 1722 Daniel Defoe mentions the nearby town Walton calling it "Walton, under the Nase", no longer under, but now Walton-on-the-Naze.

Frinton-on-Sea

Frinton-on-Sea is a small seaside town in Essex, in the Tendring district. Boasting a reputation as an exclusive resort, Frinton retains an atmosphere of the 1920s into the 30s. Tree-lined residential avenues sweep down towards elegant Esplanade and the cliff-top greensward. The whole area was later purchased by a developer with a view to building an exclusive seaside town, a quiet place with sands and some fantastic Art Deco buildings, quaint shops and restaurants in tree-lined avenues.

The Old Parish Church of St. Mary, Frinton-on-Sea

The smallest complete parish church in in Essex of Norman origin.

The primary shopping street Connaught Avenue named after the Duke of Connaught and was opened by his wife; has since been dubbed the "Bond Street" of East Anglia that runs from The Gates – railway crossing - towards the sea-front. Pubs and fish and chip shops where banned until 2000. Frinton was the last target in England to be attacked by the German Luftwaffe in 1944.

The Original Frinton Art Deco House

During the 1920's architect Oliver Hill planned to develop a luxury Art Deco Estate involving a prospective 100 room cliff top hotel, cinema, colleges, churches and houses all depicting the elegant Art Deco Designs of the Twenties. Sadly, lack of funding or demand for these way out designs called a halt to the development, and along with the outbreak of war in 1939 ended Oliver Hills vision, resulting in the company being dissolved.

The completely round 'Estate Office' remains today with an impressive mosaic floor showing the plans of the intended estate (not open to the public). The dozen or so Art Deco houses continue to be lived in to this day, and are well worth a visit to this part of Frinton, new houses in Deco style are now being built in this area.

Frinton has only two points of entry by road, one being an un-adopted road coming from Walton-on-the-Naze at the north and the other passing the railway gates at the level crossing with the town's railway station. Living "inside The Gates" is considered by some, more exclusive than living outside. Once geographically distinct, a series of housing estate now join Frinton and its neighbours: Walton-on-the-Naze to the North East, the villages of Kirby Cross and Kirby-Le-Soken to the West.

The old railway gates at Frinton

The Gates where never classified as a listed building, despite an appeal by the town council. The national organisation that recommends structures to be listed said the gates did not qualify as they were not old enough, even though they appear on the town council's coat of arms

In 2008 the town was on a campaign to "Save Frinton Gates", but in spite of the three yearlong campaign by the town's people to save the gates, at 2am on Saturday 18 April 2009, Network Rail replaced the old wooden gates on the level crossing at the entrance to Frinton with modern remotely operated lifting barriers. Network Rail did this in order to improve performance and safety, and to reduce costs. The morning following the gates' removal, around a hundred people gathered to protest strongly over the decision.

Frinton is unique, with its attractive coastal location commanding sea views, being a source of great delight and pride to the locals who fight to preserve the era of the quaint seaside spirit that is unequalled in the UK.

Radio Caroline

MV Ross Revenge, home of Radio Caroline from 1983

In 1964 Ronan O'Rahilly purchased a ship to be anchored 3 miles off the coast, as a radio ship which he called Radio Caroline. The frequency was announced of "199" wavelength, which rhymed with "Caroline". This pioneer of commercial radio was to broadcast at sea from the vessel Mi Amigo. The first Caroline began broadcasting on Easter Sunday, but was joined a month later on May 9 by a second ship to start pop radio called Radio Atlanta which anchored 3 miles off the Essex coast.

Behind the scenes talks were going on to make the links stronger and effect a merger. This took place in July of the same year, and soon Caroline steamed off to the Isle of Man to tap into an untouched audience, while Atlanta changed names to became Radio Caroline.

Both ships are fitted with special anchoring equipment to weather the storms. Normally there are two anchors in use, but when the weather turns bad only one heavy-duty anchor was used and the ship can then sail out the storm, circling the anchor. That's one spin the DJ's say they can well do without!

The format of those pirate radio was influenced by Radio Luxembourg and American radio stations. Many followed a top 40 pop record chart with DJs like Tony Blackburn. A number of DJs of the first BBC pop music station called Radio 1 came from the pirate stations.

Radio Caroline's first programme, on 28 March 1964, was presented by Chris Moore. Presenters Tony Blackburn, Roger Day, Simon Dee, Tony Prince, Spangles Muldoon, Johnnie Walker, Robbie Dale, Dave Lee Travis, Tommy Vance, Paul Noble, Bob Stewart and Andy Archer became well known. Some DJs from the USA and Commonwealth countries, such as Graham Webb, Tom Lodge, Emperor Rosko, Steve Young, Colin Nicol and Norman St John, were also heard. DJ Jack Spector, of the WMCA "Good Guys" in New York, regularly recorded for Radio Caroline. Syndicated shows from the US and recorded religious programmes were also broadcast. BBC Radio 2 newsreader Colin Berry and Classic FM's Nick Bailey started their careers reading the news on Radio Caroline South.

Clacton on Sea to Walton on the Naze - Walk 1

Clacton Sea Front

This is a very enjoyable walk along the sea wall from Clacton to Walton on the Naze. The sea wall is largely below street level in the built up areas so there is little traffic noise. However once past the residential area, the sea wall is higher than the adjoining land, so that there are beautiful views across Holland Haven Country Park. From the beach huts of Frinton you can - tides permitting - walk along the splendid firm sandy beach all the way to the town of Walton. Just past a radio mast you may spot a bird hide inland, by a lake, which by a short detour is worth a visit.

Clacton to Walton

Distance: 7 miles

Time taken: 3½ hours

Location: Clacton on Sea coastal path

OS Explorer Map: 184

Grid Reference: TM 184 150

Parking: Thorpe-le-Soken Rail Station (for trains from Walton, and to Clacton)

Bus 3 or 4 to Clacton Pier, and 105,107,109 from Walton to Colchester, via Thorpe le Soken. Hourly buses number 7, 7X, or 8 which run from Walton-on-the-Naze back to Clacton-on-Sea.

Train: Liverpool St. - Colchester - Clacton-on-Sea, returning from Walton-on-the-Naze via Thorpe le Soken.

There are refreshments available at several beach kiosks along the route. At the time of writing there is a vast coast protection scheme in action between Holland on Sea and Clacton, which is often visually great, but sometime impairing.

Grayson Perry a House for Essex. Holbrooke across the Stour

A House for Essex is designed by Grayson Perry and FAT Architecture. It is both an artwork in itself and the setting for a number of works by Grayson Perry discovering the special character and unique qualities of Essex. The building has been designed to induce a tradition of wayside and pilgrimage chapels. It belongs to a history of follies, whilst also being profoundly of its own time.

A House for Essex was featured in Channel 4 documentary - Grayson Perry's Dream House. Perry has described the building, which stands alone among the rolling fields of rural north Essex, as the Taj Mahal on the river Stour because it tells the (fictional) story of a local woman, Julie, whose husband had the house built as a shrine on her death.

Walton-on-the-Naze - Walk 2

Distance is about 3 miles - allow around:2 hours 30 minutes.

A large part of the walk is on grass but is accessible for wheelchairs or buggies. Part of the walk also takes you by the crumbling cliff edge where extreme care should be taken.

Walton-on-the-Naze is one of the most recognisable areas in Essex, although due to the sea it is constantly changing.

Make your way over to the Naze Tower and use this time to view the sea and Naze Tower. This is a circular walk starting and finishing at the historic tower, taking in some of the sights and sounds of the seaside town. Discover the history of the Naze and Walton Town and see some of the big vistas of unspoilt countryside and sea vistas in Essex.

Parking is available in the Naze car park (charges apply) or a nearby street if available.

Walking map below

Stage 1 The Naze Tower (great for a cuppa with view)

Stage 2 Fossil Cliffs (The path here is now more inland due to cliff erosion)

Stage 3 John Weston Nature Reserve (good to spot the wildlife)

Stage 4 Walton Backwaters

Stage 5 The Foundry

Stage 6 Walton Town and Naze Park

Stage 7 Walton Coastguard Station and Maritime Museum

Stage 8 Walton beach

4. Clacton-on-Sea

Clacton-on-Sea faces due south in a gently curving bay of beautiful sands. Within its boundaries are residential Holland-on-Sea to the east and Jaywick to the west, in addition to its attractive location it has a very dry and sunny climate. Clacton is a health and pleasure resort. It has merited the distinction of being Britain's least rainfall holiday town for two consecutive summers. The helter-skelter above blew down in the 2014 gale, it is hoped for a reconstruction of this iconic tower, but maybe the structure is too damaged.

The Waverley Steam Paddle Ship arriving at Clacton Pier on the way to Southend on Sea and then on to London where it passes under the raised Tower Bridge.

Fishing off Clacton Pier Digital Art by Doug Carpenter

Clacton on Sea 1897

Clacton is a popular east-coast seaside town, it experiences a fine dry climate, plus a healthy sea breeze. It owes its development principally to the introduction of the railway in 1882, since which it has rapidly expanded. The town lies high on the cliff, and the firm yellow sand make the bathing remarkably good. The pier is about a quarter of a mile long, and still is one of the points of call for the fine Clyde-built steamer "The Waverley" which run in the summer to and from London, Clacton is a clean looking town, and has its ephemeral summer visitors, who enjoy the hotels, many B&B's, pubs, café and restaurant's.

Water Amusement where there used to be Underground Toilets

Clacton Town is well laid out with tree-lined streets, modern shopping centre, and a pleasant sea-front which is largely unspoiled by tower blocks.

Visitors may be both delighted and refreshed by the brightness and colour of the attractively landscaped sea-front gardens. Exotic palm trees, Chinese Sunken Garden and the exotic shrub covered cliffs top to heighten the pleasure of a walk along the Marine promenade's fashionable and picturesque cliff top gardens, which overlooks the lovely sandy beach and pier.

Clacton on Sea 1920's Flower Gardens

Clacton Chinese Flower Garden in the snow

This garden uses around 10,000 colourful bedding plants in both spring and summer and the banks are clothed in ground cover plants and specimen shrubs. The centre piece of this garden is a sundial on a brick plinth.

Clacton Pier Slide which blew down in the 2014 Gale

Clacton's famous pier was built in 1877 and attracts families with its vast range of traditional seaside entertainments, much of which are under cover. A sandy beach considered child friendly with local lifeguard patrol and first aid cover. Adjacent and to the South, Martello Tower Beach is another sandy beach named after a small defensive fort known as a 'Martello Tower', which dates back to the nineteenth century. Plenty of facilities including beach huts, coffee bars, putting green and the Martello Pub are accessible from the beach.

The Yorkshire Pierrots Performed at the West Cliff Beach

Fred Pullan's Yorkshire-based touring troupe opened in Clacton in 1901, providing seaside entertainment, located on a small stage on stilts located on the beach. With a piano on stage for music, a portrait hung on the rear wall as a backdrop. The women in the audience often wear long skirts, dresses and hats. There was a small selection of shops providing tea and cakes, along the walkway. The show came to an end when a gale destroyed the stage in August 1912. Notice the row of bathing huts along the beach, these are the forerunners of today's beach huts selling for thousands of pounds.

Great and Little Holland

The two parishes of Great and Little Holland lie along the Essex coast, between Walton and Clacton, amid natural conditions similar to those of the Netherland on the opposite side of the North Sea. The low lying marshes, the habitat of innumerable aquatic birds, are protected against encroachments of the sea by an extensive range of embankments, kept up by local commissioners appointed under the authority of Parliament.

Great Holland All Saints

The church consists of chancel and nave, with north aisle of four bays, and an embattled brick tower. The two old fifteenth century bells remain, inscribed respectively: Omnes Sancti orate pro nobis. Amen; and Vox Augustini Sonet in aure Dei. Most of the fabric was rebuilt in the early English style in 1866, the aisle being an addition of that year.

Clacton-on-Sea Lifeboat Station - RNLI

Clacton old Lifeboat Station on the Pier

Clacton-on-Sea new Lifeboat Station is a Discover station. There is normally much activity to watch on Sunday morning when they open their boathouse doors during the summer months for visitors. Clacton-on-Sea lifeboat was one of the 19 lifeboats that took part in the evacuation of the British Expeditionary Force from Dunkirk. Celebrating over 125 years of saving lives at sea the crews have been presented with over 30 awards for gallantry. In 1878 Clacton received its first official lifeboat, a gift of the Freemasons. It was named Albert Edwards, after the Royal Prince at that time. In 1886, two slipways were cut either side of the pier. The lifeboat was then kept on the pier during the winter months.

Launching the new lifeboat Ess065 type RP 1936

Clacton Pier, which was the first building of the new resort of Clacton-on-Sea. It officially opened on 27 July 1871 and was 480 feet in length and 12 feet wide. The pier was originally built as a docking point for goods and passengers, but soon became popular for promenading.

New hi-tech Clacton-on-Sea Lifeboat

By the 1890s Clacton was becoming an increasingly favourite destination for day trippers and in 1893 the pier was lengthened to 1180 feet (360m), to allow steamers and boat to dock at all states of the tide. In1936 a lifeboat extension was built on the side of the pier, which save the time it took to push the old boat from across the road.

Clacton Coastguard Station, near to The Martello Tower D

Clacton Coastguard, responsible for search and rescue at sea along our coast, is stationed at Hastings Avenue, Clacton-on-Sea, CO15 1BW. Telephone: 01255 421471

The Coastguard has had a variety of different responsibilities, ranging from those laid down in the Coastguard Service Act 1856. Namely to provide for the defence of the coasts of the realm, the emergency manning of the Royal Navy in the event of war, and the protection of the revenue, to assisting vessels in distress, taking charge of wrecks, operating life-saving apparatus, participating in the lifeboat service, searching for mines and torpedoes lost at sea, and performing sundry duties in connection with signals, buoys, lighthouses, wild birds and rare fish or mammals washed ashore.

The Coastguard when run by the Admiralty consisted of three distinct bodies; the Shore Force, the Permanent Cruiser Force and the Guard Ships, naval ships which lay at major ports to act as headquarters of Coastguard districts.

After the First World War there was a significant reduction in the manpower of the Coastguard Service. Control of the Service changed hands 5 times after 1923:

Board of Trade 1923-1939
Ministry of Shipping 1939-1940
Admiralty 1940-1945
Ministry of (War Transport 1945-1964
Department of Trade 1964-1983
Department for the Environment, Transport and the Regions.

Jaywick Sands

Jaywick probably a dairy farm in saxon times, named along the lines of: Clacton-inga-wick then became Clacton-jewick and over time shortened to Jaywick. The land was sold by the lords of the manor to pay off their debts. Lady Elizabeth Savage was one of the owners who sold to a then new type of business person, Mr John Langham from London.

Martello Tower at Jaywick now an exhibition centre and observation tower

Typical Jaywick Street Today and Past Times

In 1928 Frank Stedman purchased Jaywick marshlands; he had dreams of a seaside centre and village. Stedman proceeded to build 5 chalets in Golf Green Road then the beach hut section at the lower end of Meadow Way. Later that year Stedman began the building of Brooklands called Jaywick Sands Estate, the plots cost £45 and bungalows cost up to £350, with roads names after cars brands like; Sunbeam, Wolseley, Humber and Bentley Avenue.

Jaywick and Clacton East now part of Clacton town, complete with its own buses, shops, amusements and sports grounds, it even had a miniature railway at the Crossways for around three years.

The small part of town has suffered four major floods, the first in 1936, 1948 and 1949. But by far the worse in 1953; the east coast was hit by a massive storm and 35 people in Jaywick lost their lives. Fortunately, the last big storm in 2013 put to the test the new sea defences - which some would say – was very successful. Picture below The Martello Tower D looking towards Clacton Pier

Notice on the Beach, Jaywick Sands

St Osyth

St. Osyth boasts England's most haunted houses "The Cage" was once a medieval prison and housed many women, including England's most ill-famed witch Ursula Kemp, who was accused of witchcraft and hanged in 1582. Ursula a young nursemaid and healer, was well known by the local folk for her special ability of removing curses, and for making and selling potions to cure the sick. She was said to be a fine woman and a good mother to her son. After a local woman accused Ursula of witchcraft and went to Lord Brian Darcy of St Osyth Priory with her complaint, the notorious St. Osyth witch trials began, ending in the poor women's death.

St Osyth's Priory Gatehouse

At St. Osyth the chief interest of the place lies in the history of St. Osyth's Priory, extensive remains of which are preserved in the house and grounds that occupy the site. The traditional account may be summarized as follows: In early times the manor, then known as Chich, was given by Sighere, King of the East Saxons, to his wife Osyth, who their established a nunnery. In or about 870 the Danes sacked the house, and, on their offering the lady the usual alternative, she preferred martyrdom to apostasy, and was beheaded.

To this day a spring is pointed out as the scene of her passion, where the water miraculously burst forth as her head fell to the ground. The story goes on to say that she speedily arose, and carried her head to the church, where her body was eventually deposited. She was afterwards canonized, and an Austin Priory (soon converted into an Abbey) was founded there by Richard de Belmeis I, Bishop of London (1108-28), with a dedication to her honour, in conjunction with Saints Peter and Paul.

After the suppression, the monastery, with most of its property, was granted by Henry VIII to Thomas Cromwell, on whose attainder the estate reverted to the Crown, and was sold to Thomas Lord D'Arcy in 1553. He soon set to work to convert the ancient pile into the spacious mansion of red brick and stone which we now see, with the additions made to it by his successors, and such of the earlier structure as has been preserved, notably the stately entrance gateway, and most of the original quadrangle, surrounded by a well timbered park of 250 acres.

St. Osyth Boatyard

The church retains the old dedication (Saints Osyth, Peter, and Paul), and consists of chancel with chapels, nave with aisles, and massive west tower containing six bells. Most of the fabric is of fifteenth-century date, but contains some good modern work in the stained windows, etc. A remarkable feature is the arrangement of the sanctuary railing in the form of a horseshoe, locally known as " The Fold," with an interesting significance which speaks for itself. There are numerous monuments to the D'Arcy family and other distinguished residents of the sixteenth and seventeenth centuries, some bearing recumbent effigies.

Fishing Smack CK 273 at St Osyth's Creek

The Edme Thames barge sails out of St. Osyth's Creek, maintained and docks at the boat yard. The Edme a 50 ton, built of wood at Harwich in 1898 by Cann and owned by F.W. Horlock. De-rigged for use as a lighter 1949 by Brown & Co. After a lengthy restoration at Maldon she was bought by the Harman-Harrison Consortium, and now the Edme Consortium. Re-rigged as a bowsprit barge in 1992, based at St. Osyth's. She is the only Thames barge that has no engine. You may also find the Essex fishing smack CK273 and a torpedo boat plus many other boats in varying states of repair at this characterful Creek.

Blackwater Estuary

Blackwater is the largest estuary in Essex and a great place to get a real sense of coastal wilderness. The reserve is split into 3 main areas: Old Hall Marshes, Tollesbury Flats and Salcott Flats.

Access to Old Hall Marshes is free, but donations are welcomed and opening times are between 9 am-9 pm or dusk.

The Tollesbury and Salcott Flats are intertidal mud and sand flats, which are exposed at low water. This part of the reserve is closed to the public as it is a sensitive intertidal zone. However, you can view the mudflats from the adjacent sea wall.

Main habitats: mudflats, salt marsh, grazing marsh, reedbeds, fresh water, intertidal mud and sand. Management: Royal Society for Protection of Birds (RSPB) and Natural England

Old Hall Marshes

These marshes are home to a range of breeding and over-wintering waterfowl. It is estimated that 4000 Brent geese feed on the marshes in winter, along with other waterfowl such as teal and shelduck. A population of bearded tits enjoys areas of reed bed. The site also supports a number of nationally important plant and invertebrate species, including 24 species of butterfly, along with dragon and damselflies, most notably the rare emerald damselfly.

A recent survey showed that Tollesbury Flats are the richest area of the Blackwater for its diverse invertebrate populations. These mudflats are a very essential area for native oysters, which explains why it is also a good place to spot the dramatic red-beaked oystercatchers especially when in flight and flickering black and white in the sunlight.

Light boat training boat in the Blackwater Estuary

The tidal mudflats of both Salcott and Tollesbury are superior feeding grounds for other waders, such as curlew, redshank, dunlin and greenshank, and waterfowl such as wigeon and goldeneye. In winter time, these are great areas for spotting migrants from northern Europe, such as grey plover, ruff and birds of prey like the hen harriers.

5. Brightlingsea - Wivenhoe - Point Clear

Point Clear from Brightlingsea

Brightlingsea a maritime English heritage town is well-known for its beach huts and sailing clubs. Brightlingsea is a coastal town within the Tendring district of Essex, England, situated at the mouth of the River Colne on Brightlingsea Creek between Colchester and Clacton-on-Sea. It has an estimated population of 8500. Its conventional industries included fishery and shipbuilding. Using the decline of these industries, the town is largely a dormitory town for Colchester, and a popular retirement destination.

In the centre of the Brightlingsea town is Jacobs Hall, regarded as the oldest timber-framed building in England, built during the fourteenth century. West of town on the creek is Western Promenade. It has many of the much loved beach huts, a sculptural skate park, open air swimming pool, fabulous boating lake, and children's paddling pool.

Bateman's Tower Brightlingsea (Digital Art)

The Tower built in 1883 by John Bateman as a folly for his daughter to recuperate from consumption. The tower is situated on Westmarsh Point on the River Colne at the entrance to Brightlingsea Creek. Bateman's Tower, has recently been renovated by the Colne Yacht Club with help from a Lottery Fund grant.

Point Clear looking towards Mersea Island

Point Clear is a small village in the civil parish of St Osyth in the Tendring district. Made up of many holiday home and caravans, but very characterful and well worth a walk around.

Just south of Point Clear is Colne Point Nature Reserve This large and important 683 acre reserve at the mouth of the Colne Estuary and consists of a shingle ridge enclosing a considerable area of saltmarsh, through which Ray Creek flows. It is an important nesting site for Little Terns. A very difficult to get to area.

Point Clear looking toward Colne Point

The Cinque Port Liberty

Before the Norman Conquest, King Edward the Confessor had contracted the 5 most vital Channel ports of that day to provide ships and men "for the service of the monarch" under the Norman kings but immediately after the loss of Normandy in 1205, the ships suddenly became England's first line of defence against the French.

Today the Cinque Ports have only a ceremonial function, but a base for the Lord Warden of the Ports continues to be appointed at Walmer Castle and new Lords Warden are always installed at Dover, Kent.

All members of the Confederation, together with their Limbs, are situated in Kent or Sussex, apart from Brightlingsea which, as a Limb of Sandwich, uniquely lies in Essex.

By Brightlingsea becoming a Limb of Sandwich it could contribute to that town's ship-service quota. For the Lord Warden, it made sense extending his powers so far north of Sussex and Kent over the total width of the mouth of the Thames. Also it produced excellent oysters and the Lord Warden had his own official oyster beds in Brightlingsea Creek until at least the 1670's. The town retains an active ceremonial connection with the Cinque Ports, electing a Deputy from a Guild of Freemen.

Thames Sailing Barge Edme

Brightlingsea is abound in maritime history. Excavations in the past discovered a major Bronze Age burial site, these settlers drawn in by a plentiful supply of fish and fresh water. A Roman fort on the river at Brightlingsea formed a part of the defences for Colchester. In the 18th and 19th centuries Brightlingsea was famous for its sprats, sold as far afield as Russia, and the harbour was alive with a large fleet of fishing boats. The fleet is sadly no more but some of the old smacks, which fished under sail, have been lovingly restored and are popular in the harbour.

Events around Brightlingsea throughout the year: In June the Town Regatta and boat show takes place. Later in the month the carnival, with floats that capture the fun of the fair. In August the well-attended music festival draws the crowds in over the four-day event. Just down the road Pyefleet Week takes place, run by Brightlingsea sailing club. August finishes with the Town Show, which is horticulture craft and a dog show.

Come September there is usually a classic car show. The highlight of the month, maybe is the Smack and Barge race, which starts around 8 am the annual race is still held, usually on the second Saturday in September, for the coveted "Cock of the Colne" trophy. It's quite a sight to see 20 smacks and a dozen Thames barges head out of the River Colne towards Clacton-on-Sea.

The year comes to triumphant end with the Christmas Tree Festival at All Saints Church. All subject to change, look in the local press for details.

Fishing Smack beached for the Winter

The top main mast of the barge is down to resist storm damage, and a fishing Smack between Brightlingsea and Point Clear sails passed.

Brightlingsea Town Hard and Causeway

The Town Hard given by the late William Pannell in 1898 and still much in use today. There is a new black marble monument to the Olympic gold medalist Reg White (1935-2010) to be found near the entrance of the pier.

Brightlingsea has a sandy beach backed by a promenade lined with colourful beach huts, plus an open air swimming pool and nearby model yachting lake. Brightlingsea is now a haven for yachting. Formerly an important fishing and shipbuilding area now a popular resort with plenty of amenities, indeed a seaside with a enjoyable difference!

Crabbing off Brightlingsea Pier

Crabbing is great family fun and crabbing kits, which includes pieces of chicken or bacon, a hook, and plenty of string, plus a net with a 3 or 4-foot pole and a bucket for the catch can be purchase in local shops.

Brightlingsea Town Regatta and Boat Show will be held on an early weekend in July. The shipyard estate is the base for the Marine's Boat Show, with exhibitors showing new and used motor and sailing boats and stallholders featuring canopies, GRP repairers, electronics, chandlery, trailers, sailmakers and more. The Boat show runs from 10am to 5pm on both days, entrance is free and there's a Park and Ride too. The Shipyard Estate will also be the base for a continental market, while on the Hard there'll be craft stalls, art on the railings, music, crabbing for the children and stalls promoting local organisations.

Brightlingsea Town Regatta

The nearby Marina will also feature music and stalls, with more on Fieldgate Dock. The Regatta events will be taking place in front of the Colne Yacht Club on the waterfront between 1pm to 5pm. At the sailing club you can try dinghy sailing, or keep your feet dry and watch the Model Boat Club displays on the boating lake.

All Saints' Church and the lychgate, Brightlingsea

All Saints' Church built c.1250 incorporates part of an earlier building and much Roman brickwork. The Baptistery under the tower include a fine Tudor font look for traces of the original paintwork and the original West door. The Chancel holds an ornate marble memorial to Nicholas Magens, an 18th Century Lord of the Manor, underwriter and merchant. The Church is manned by custodians most afternoons.

The Church is the older church in Brightlingsea and is a grade 1 listed building dating back to the 12th century and set in a six-acre churchyard. It is well maintained and is the venue for the majority of weddings and funerals. It is right on the borders of the parish and perched on a hill so can be seen for miles. This parish church is held in much affection by the townspeople and is used regularly for worship and events like the Christmas tree festival.

A unique feature of All Saints' Church is the frieze in which are set some 212 tiles, each one bearing the name of a Brightlingsea man lost at sea since the year 1872, together with the name of the ship on which they served. The memorial was the idea of the Reverend Arthur Pertwee the vicar of Brightlingsea, after the tragic loss of 36 men of the fishing fleet that year in severe storms in the North Sea.

The other church being The Parish of All Saints with St James which is in the town centre.

Brightlingsea Open Air Pool

Brightlingsea Open Air Pool on Promenade Way, was originally built in 1933, and comprises two pools, a 15m paddling pool and a 50m main pool. Once a salt water pool, this is now a two level freshwater lido facility and is one of the few remaining outdoor swimming pools left in the UK. It is very popular with local residents and holidaymakers alike.

Brightlingsea Town changing display

Wyvenhoe Thames Sailing Barge

Wivenhoe Town

Wivenhoe is a town and civil parish on the banks of the River Colne, approximately 3 miles (4.8 km) south east of Colchester and north east of Brightlingsea. Historically Wivenhoe village, and Wivenhoe Cross, on the higher ground to the north, were two separate settlements but with considerable development in the 19th century the two have merged. Wivenhoe also has much by way of designated conservation area, with many buildings being of particular architectural interest.

Wivenhoe history involves fishing, yachts, ships and smuggling; a pretty church, with a distinctive cupola on top of its sturdy tower, stands on the site of the first church, built in Saxon times. The streets are small and quaint, leading into each other and ending at the picturesque waterfront where fishing boats and small sailing craft bob at their moorings.

The Port of Wivenhoe until the late 19th century was the port for Colchester, as large ships were unable to navigate any further up the River Colne.

Wyvenhoe Sailing Barge was built of iron in 1898, at Wivenhoe in Essex. Like most Thames sailing barges, she was rigged with a spritsail rig which enabled a small crew of two or three men to handle her. She was converted to a motor ship in 1923, and after being rebuilt in steel in 1947, she traded until 1982. She holds the record of having traded longer than any other British registered ship. Length 85 feet, Beam 19 feet, Draught about 4 feet. Registered tonnage of 83.19 tons. Sail area: 3,500 square feet with traditional sails, treated with red-ochre and linseed oil, a treat to watch.

A charter aboard Wyvenhoe is an ideal opportunity for artists and photographers to gain a unique perspective of the creeks and rivers of the Essex coast.

Wivenhoe from across the River Colne - Digital Art

Wyvenhoe's Skipper is Martin Phillips. An enthusiast of Thames Barges, he has been sailing for over 40 years and was a regular mate on charter barges for 25 years.

The Riverside villages of Rowhedge and Wivenhoe have a rich maritime heritage. Generations of shipwrights, sailors, racing-yacht captains and crew, sail-makers and fishermen have come from these villages.

Wivenhoe Walk

Landing stage in Alresford Creek Digital Watercolour

This walk takes you along the picturesque waterfront of Wivenhoe, alongside the quay with characterful fishing boats, and out into the panoramic riverside with vast skies alongside the River Colne. It passes over the marshland, now grazed by cattle, along the old Wivenhoe to Brightlingsea railway line, and returns via an avenue of trees with marvellous views of the estuary from higher up. The bird songs along the route are a delight to the ear in the ancient woodland boundary of Arlesford Grange, before returning along the sea wall for refreshments on the quayside at the Rose and Crown Pub, the perfect way to relax after a walk, with a splendid vista across to Rowhedge.

Distance: 3½ miles or turn around and walk back at will. Time taken: 1½ hours

Parking: NCP Wivenhoe Station CO7 9DJ Bus: Regular buses or train from Colchester

Wivenhoe's name comes from a Saxon farmer named Wiffa, who settled here sometime after the Romans left Britain in 410AD. A Hoe is a ridge, so this is Wiffa's hoe. Wivenhoe is mentioned in the Domesday Book in 1086.

Boat building has taken place at Wivenhoe since 1575 and has seen shipyards building fishing smacks, cargo vessels, minesweepers and MTBs. One of the last vessels built was the sail training ship, The Lord Nelson. Wivenhoe is a pretty East Coast town with riverside pubs alongside the mud berths and moorings.

St Mary-the-Virgin parish church was largely restored and enlarged after a serious fire in 1850. The tower dates from 1500, and the unusual Georgian cupola was added in 1734. Every year on the first Saturday in June they have a very popular event 'Art on the Railings', when local artists hang their pictures for sale all-round the churchyard railings.

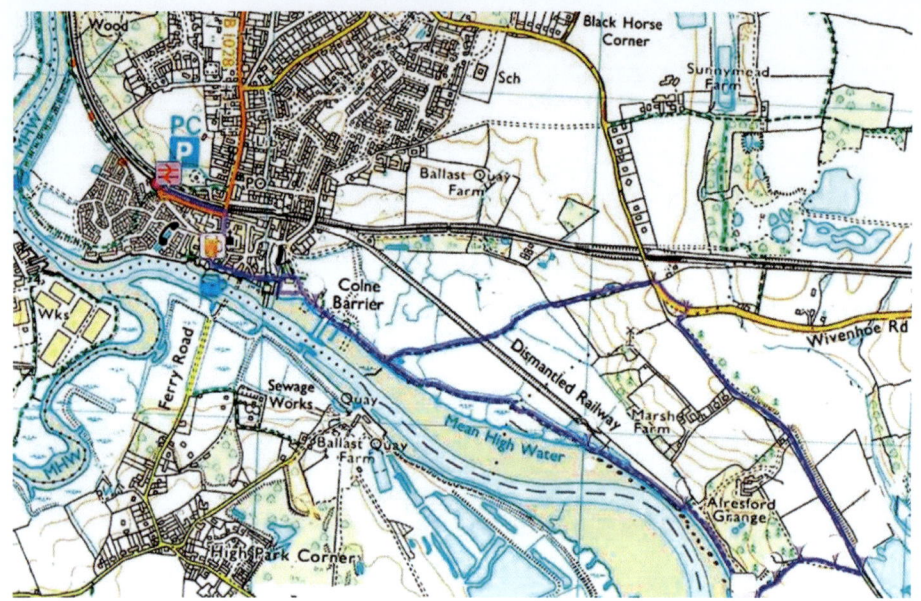

Garrison House, built in the early 17th century, is one of the finest examples of the decorative plasterwork, called pargetting, in the country, built as a meeting hall originally. It is called Garrison House because it is said to have been occupied by Parliamentarian officers during the English Civil War siege of Colchester, which lasted for nearly three months in the summer of 1648.

The railway came to Wivenhoe in 1863 and the Station Hotel public house followed. The trees on the other side of the tracks are Wivenhoe Woods. A few minutes along the path is Ferry Marsh, a nature reserve with mown grass paths leading through reed beds to the waterside, giving pleasant views across the river to Rowhedge.

Wivenhoe Sailing Club founded in 1925, moved to the top floor of the three-storey building on the corner. The local branch of the Royal British Legion hold their meetings and social events on the ground floor. The building was once used for sail making.

Fishing Smack moored at Wivenhoe MN = Maldon registered

A very popular ferry service is run from here on summer weekends. Passengers can go to The Anchor at Rowhedge, or across to Fingringhoe, or take a round trip. The ferry is managed by a charitable trust and staffed by volunteers.

A housing estate is built on the site of the former major shipbuilding beside the port area. This was a wharf where in the old days the fishing boats would discharge their catch to be taken to London on the railway. In the 19th century Wivenhoe was a famous yachting centre. Edward, Prince of Wales had two boats built here which were crewed by local men.

Harding's Yard by the quay, is now mews type houses with artistic gardens. Before being converted recently this was the Colne Marine and Yacht Company yard, and over twenty large yachts were launched from here, the longest being a fifty-one footer.

Wivenhoe's downriver shipyard is now a housing estate; ships were built on this site from the 1840's until 1986. James Cook and Company Limited was the last company here; they came after the second world war. They built all kinds of specialised craft, including the largest sailing ship to be built in the UK for seventy-five years, the 140-ton square rig schooner "The Lord Nelson".

The ford crossing Alresford Creek (Digital Art)

There's a pleasant riverside walk along part of the old Brightlingsea to Wivenhoe railway track. The River Colne and Brightlingsea Creek, plus Pyfleet Creek lies to the west and offers a popular anchorage. The ruined pier at Fingringhoe on the western bank and the Colne channel bends to the north. Alresford creek branches to the east. The commercial wharf at Ballast Quay is near the Wivenhoe tidal barrier.

Rowhedge has pritty riverside gardens and houses with characterful boats at its moorings. The town provided many of the yacht crews for the gentry in times past. The Anchor pub has a ladder on the sea wall allowing access from the river.

Rowhedge is on the right bank of the tidal River Colne and is the first settlement downstream, about 4 km (2.5 miles) from Colchester. The history of Rowhedge is connected directly to the River Colne's ship and boat building bygone age.

The Rowhedge Regatta is an annual event held in June. A family event with many quayside activities including greasy pole, art and craft stalls, BBQ and other food stalls, fancy dress competition, fun dog show, belly dancers, Morris men, brass band, samba band, African drumming and crabbing competition, and the spectacular sight of the fishing smack boats arriving in front of the crowds gathered on the quayside.

Brightlingsea Point Clear East Mersea Foot Ferry

Foot ferry passing Batman's Tower on the way to Mersea Island

The Ferry provides not only a means of crossing the creek, but opens up opportunities to explore the attractions and facilities the area has to offer such as Cudmore Grove Country Park.

The custom built ferry boat has a ramp which can be lowered to allow easy access for wheelchair users and cycles, as well as foot passengers using the service.

Use of the ferry greatly reduces road miles - typically a round trip by road between Brightlingsea and Point Clear is 20 miles, but takes just 3 minutes on the ferry. The round trip by road to East Mersea is 40 miles, but only takes approximately 9 minutes by ferry.

Scheduled service:

Brightlingsea – Point Clear – Brightlingsea

On demand except when the ferry is crossing to East Mersea

Brightlingsea – East Mersea – Brightlingsea

Three scheduled crossings each day, although additional crossings can be provided on request.

Depart from Brightlingsea to Point Clear then East Mersea on the hour between 10.00 and

16.00 (last crossing) when booked prior to the departure time - the Ferry will only run when it has been booked.

Boat graveyard near Pointclear

The peculiar part of the Essex coast is flat, marshy and is served by a number of small streams and creeks of little note in literature, and generally meandering in appearance.

6 Mersea

Mersea is reached by crossing the dramatic Strood causeway, not always possible at high tide, and you may be stranded on the Island until the tide recedes. Mersea is a renowned oyster producer and there are still many oyster beds to be spotted on the River Colne.

Mersea Oyster Shed River Colne

The picturesque island of Mersea, between the estuaries of the Colne and Blackwater, is oval in shape, about five miles in length, and two miles in its widest part, rising in the interior to a considerable height above the sea level, and sinking gradually towards the flat marshes and saltings which stretch around the coast.

Mersea Island was granted in 1046 by Edward the Confessor to the Abbey of St. Ouen at Rouen, and a small priory was founded here in consequence close to the site of the present church. Suppressed as an alien house by Henry V, the property was transferred to Archbishop Chicheley, in aid of the College which he was founding at Higham Ferrers, and the monastic building has long since disappeared.

Mersea Island is actually situated inside the estuary area with the Blackwater and Colne rivers and has an area of about 8 square kilometres divided into two areas East and West.

The West is served by a community centre, various shops, restaurants, small hotels, public houses, a petrol station, bank, library, police station and several churches, including St Peter and St Paul, which is Norman and Church of England. Plus, Roman Catholic, Methodist and the Evangelical Free Church.

The island is surrounded by oyster rich water and has provided the famous Colchester oysters since Roman times. Oysters from the River Blackwater, to the west of the Island, have been cultivated and harvested by the Haward family for seven generations, since the mid-18th century. They are a mixture of natives seasonal and wild rock oysters available all year round.

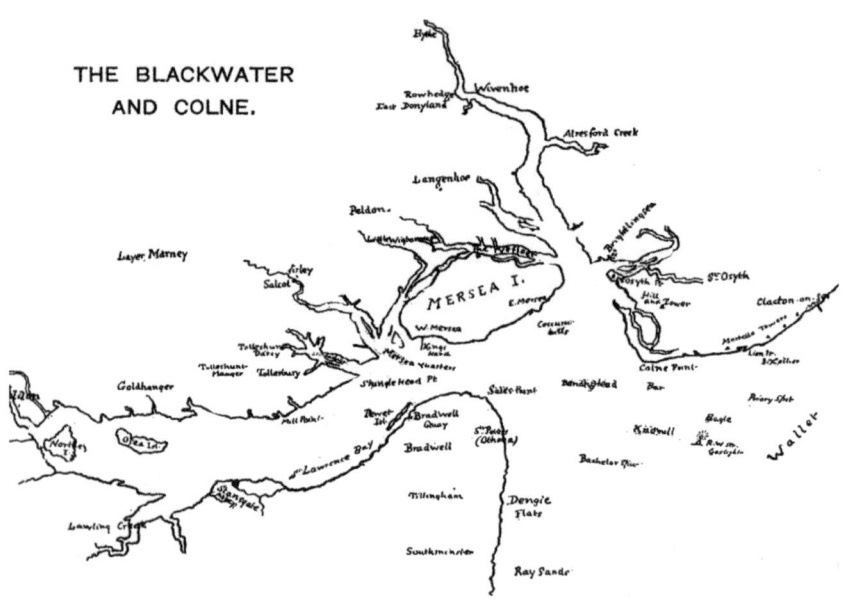

The River Colne and the Colne Estuary, to the east of the island, is the source of native and rock oysters from The Colchester Oyster Fishery, who hold the current lease on beds that were granted to the local authorities in 1189 by King Richard I, The Lionheart. Eat Colchester oysters at: The Company Shed, run by the Hawards, this is a rustic eating place that regularly receives star rated praise from all the major food critics and is usually full. Parking is very limited.

West Mersea Oyster Bar first opened its doors in 2006. In April 2010, Chris Avila as Head Chef and Sel Yuzen as Manager took over the ownership of the Oyster Bar with a modernised interior and alfresco easting.

St Peter and St Paul Church, West Mersea

The church of St Peter and St Paul is a fine Norman building of flint and stone, with much Roman tile in the walls, but considerable portions of the fabric are of later date. The most interesting and oldest part is the fine west tower, most of which is apparently even pre-Norman. The plain archway into the nave is built of Roman tiles, and the whole structure, massive as a fortress, has every sign of great antiquity. But the five bells which it contains are no older than 1717, all inscribed with that date, and the name of Thomas Gardiner of Sudbury as the founder. Note the octagonal font with basin resting on a circular shaft, once the drum of an oolite Roman pillar. There is also an interesting fifteenth century chest.

The road to Mersea Island, Essex at high spring tides

The Strood, the causeway linking Mersea to the mainland is regularly inundated at high spring tides, The Strood is itself a link to the past, for the causeway was first laid around 700 AD, when an Anglo-Saxon magnate ordered up to 5,000 oak pilings to be sunk into the underlying clay. Oak pilings don't talk, and later Viking invaders destroyed pretty well all written records in East Anglia and Essex, but one candidate as builder was the monk-king, Sæbbi of Essex, who abdicated to devote himself to prayer.

St Edmund King and Martyr Digital Art

The church on East Mersea is where the Rev. Sabine Baring Gould was Rector from 1870, he is the author of hymns including 'Onward Christian Soldiers' and 'Now the day is over' as well as 'Mehalah' a local story of violence and tragedy. The church is chiefly of fourteenth and fifteenth-century date, and stands on a declivity near the sea, at a point where the Danes are said to have taken refuge within a moated entrenchment, after their defeat by King Alfred at Farnham.

East Mersea is sparsely populated and is virtually all given over to agriculture. The Village can be a thriving with activity at Cudmore Country Park, on the picturesque island of Mersea, between the estuaries of the Colne and Blackwater, is oval in shape, about five miles in length, and two miles in its widest part, rising in the interior to a considerable height above the sea level, and sinking gradually towards the flat marshes and saltings which stretch around the coast.

The church St Edmund King and Martyr is chiefly of fourteenth and fifteenth-century date, and stands on a declivity near the sea, at a point where the Danes are said to have taken refuge within a moated entrenchment, after their defeat by King Alfred at Farnham. The embattled stone tower, formerly used for a beacon, and still a prominent land and sea mark, contains one bell (the survivor of a ring of five) inscribed Sum rosa pulsata mundi Maria vocata, cast by Richard Hille dated 1440.

The Grave of Sarah Wrench (1833-1848), by the North wall of the chancel at St. Edmund's Church is unusual for an English grave because it is covered by a mortsafe, a protective cage used at the time in Scotland to protect corpses from grave robbers. Richard Jones, in Myths of Britain and Ireland, refers to the popular speculation that Sarah Wrench was a witch, and that the cage was designed to keep her from escaping her grave after death. Although East Anglia was at one time known for witch trials, this was in the sixteenth and seventeenth centuries, not the mid-nineteenth.

East Mersea showing remains of an oyster bed

The Mersea Island Food, Drink & Leisure Festival is an event which combines the best of local food and drink with a celebration of the people and places that make Mersea Island the distinctive town it is today. Being hosted at the Mersea Island Vineyard, the festival presents local food and drink, arts, crafts, home furnishings, items for the garden, music, dance and entertainment for everybody to enjoy.

Mersea Island, River Blackwater looking towards Shinglehead Point

West Mersea looking towards Salcott cum Virley

Salcott, a small village and parish, at the head of the navigable creek in Essex and forms part of the Winstred Hundred on a creek of the Blackwater estuary, part of the land is salt marsh. A fair is held in early September. The school closed in 1937 and for many years it was used as a Church Hall. St Mary's Church is a typical looking Essex building of flint stone with a square tower and red tiled roof

Fishing Smack Pioneer looking towards Brightlingsea from East Mersea

Originally built in 1864, the 70ft Essex smack Pioneer fell into decay after a life spent dredging oysters in the North Sea. An audacious restoration project by the Pioneer Sailing Trust recovered the wreck in 1998 and restored her. Pioneer's new life as a sail training vessel can take up to 16 people and is used as a vehicle to facilitate learning skills and exploring new and adventurous territory.

Pioneer in the Strood Channel, she lay here from 1942 to 1998

Crabbing off West Mersea a popular Sunday Morning past time
Crabbing tips:

1. Crabs like raw liver, bacon, fish heads/tails, chicken or sand eels someone also suggested cat food!

2. Make sure that your bait reaches the sea bed and avoid seaweed if you can.

3. As soon as you get your crab above the water it will try to jump off. Bring your line out of the water very, very slowly.

4. Using a net can be useful to land the crabs before they jump off the line.

5. Make sure that your bucket is half full of sea water and place some seaweed in to shade and protect the crabs. Crabbing bucket and related tackle are available in the local shops.

6. Crabs don't like over-crowding - it's cruel. Current thinking is ten crabs at most, then let them go.

Mersea at Dusk Low Tide - Digital Art

7 Maldon

Maldon Prom St Mary's Church on the River Blackwater

Maldon the effective limit of upstream navigation of the River Blackwater, it's an ancient waterfront town just a stone throw away from Tollesbury and Heybridge Basin. Maldon, situated inland of the Blackwater Estuary and its sinuous landscape of meandering creeks, twisting rivers, curving borrow dykes and saltings. The picturesque town is reached on the A414 road by turning off the A12 and is signposted before Chelmsford going north. Get there by public transport - take a train to Chelmsford and cross to the bus station where there is a reasonable weekday service. At Maldon the bus stops just past the former bus station leaving a short walk to the characterful Hythe waterfront. Forking left down Church Street. Past the spired church of St Mary's dating from 1130 AD and the Jolly Sailor Pub. Other traditional industries such as barge repairing, boat building, sail making and fishing still thrive and grain is still delivered by boat at Fullbridge Quay.

Heybridge is a civil parish and large village, in the Maldon district of Essex on the River Blackwater. It is often overshadowed by its historic neighbour, and the boundaries between the two towns are lost, as the two have merged with one another over the years. There is also a place called Fullbridge which encompasses the bridge over the River Chelmer.

At a Heybridge housing estates to the west of the town, before building commenced in 1995, a full archaeological dig was undertaken and the excavations showed the existence of an important Iron Age settlement and ritual complex, a large Roman settlement and a succeeding Saxon settlement, as well as scattered pre-historic remains.

Heybridge was originally called Tidwalditun. The name Heybridge came from the high bridge that was built over the River Blackwater in the Middle Ages. This was a 5-arched stone bridge and it was replaced in 1870 by a 2-arched brick bridge. Much of the water flow down this part of the river had, by then, been diverted into the River Chelmer by diversion work done during construction of the Chelmer and Blackwater Navigation.

Maldon Prom about 1997 pencil drawing by Doug Carpenter

Probably the most popular artist image of Maldon, the scene in the Hythe with its collection of barges and other craft tied up at the quay plus the old church of St Mary the Virgin dominating the skyline.

Maldon Prom Mud Race this fun event uses to take place on Boxing Day, but has been moved to the Summer due to the extreme winter weather of late or the less hardy entrants!

Maldon Prom Mud Race Digital Art

Thames Barges in the background are flat-bottomed to make them shallow draft for getting to the very top of little creeks at high tide and for sitting on the mud as it ebbs, then flows, loading their cargo in the intervening 12 hours. In the past, the cargo was often hay to feed the horses used by the London's transport system, drawing Hackney cab people carriers, hearses, carts, carriages, brewers drays and suchlike. The horse droppings were then brought back to fertilise the crop-growing land. Perfect recycling and the pace of life and loading set by the tides in those days.

The famous Byrhtnoth statue in Maldon Promenade Park

Northey and Osea Island, Maldon

Northey is an island in the Blackwater Estuary, Essex, two miles by road from Maldon and a mile at high tide from Heybridge. The Island is mostly saltings covered at high tide. It was in these creeks that twenty-four revenue men had their throats cut in the smuggling wars and no culprits were ever found.

In the late 1940s a wild fowler Stanley Tiffin came upon a rare harvest while paddling his punt, a parcel containing the torso of a man, later identified as Stanley Shetty, a car dealer from the East End. It was a national sensation and eventually a member of Elsdon Flying Club was arrested, tried and found guilty. He had chosen to drop the body into the marshes rather than bother to fly further out to sea.

The Battle of Maldon

Here also is the site of much gory history, where 93 ships led by a certain Olaf battled their way up from Kent in AD991 and fought the Saxons under Byrhtnoth at Maldon.

Northey island is approached across a causeway and is the site of the Battle of Maldon in 991 making it Britain's oldest recorded battlefield site. The Battle took place three weeks before Whitsun 10th or maybe the 11th August 991 AD near Maldon beside the causeway to Northey Island on the shores of the River Blackwater, during the reign of Aethelred the Unready.

Earl Byrhtnoth and his legion led the English against a Viking invasion. In the battle, the Vikings, headed by Anlaf, try to land at Maldon after a series of raids along the Essex coast. The Saxons foolishly allowed the Danes to form up on Northey Island and march across the narrow wet road before engaging them in battle. Brithnoth was killed at the battle and laid to rest in Latchingdon Church. After the battle Archbishop Sigeric of Canterbury and the aldermen of the south-western provinces advised King Aethelred to buy off the Vikings rather than continue the armed struggle. The result was a payment of 10,000 Roman pounds of silver, the first example of Danegeld "Danish tax" in England.

An account of the battle, embellished with many speeches attributed to the warriors and with other details, is related in an Old English poem which is usually named The Battle of Maldon. A modern embroidery created for the millennium celebration in 1991 and, in part, depicting the battle, can be seen at the Maeldune Centre in Maldon.

This causeway is covered by sea for four hours out of every twelve. It is a site of special scientific interest with a large area of undisturbed salt marsh. Access is by advance permit only; please email northeyisland@nationaltrust.org.uk to arrange a visit. Northey Island and the adjoining South House Farm was given to the National Trust by Nora and Eric Lane in 1978.

There are only two houses on the island; the caretakers' cottage and a marvellous house in the form of a tower stands on the island, which is available for holiday letting. This is an unusual house built by a previous owner, Sir Norman Angell, winner of the Nobel Peace Prize, in the 1920's and who was great uncle to the existing tenants.

The Battle took place three weeks before Whitsun 10th or maybe the 11th August 991 AD near Maldon beside the causeway to Northey Island on the shores of the River Blackwater, during the reign of Aethelred the Unready. Nearby in the Blackwater Estuary is Osea island with 400 acres of idyllic countryside and four miles of its own beaches and coastline. Accessible only via a twisting pebble causeway, passable only every seven hours, due to the tides, the Island genuinely is an unspoilt vista of Essex.

Osea Island - a jewel in the Blackwater Estuary

Osea island has a rich and diverse history having been occupied for over 5000 years. There are remains of Neolithic villages and later evidence of Viking burial grounds from the famous battle of Maldon.

The Romans built the causeway and the salt works, a pottery and grew arable crops. With the departure of the Romans, the island passed through the hands of many powerful and titled families, emphasising its importance through to Tudor times.

Osea was purchased in Victorian times for its curative bathing and bracing sea air, the plan being to establish a colony for city alcoholics. It didn't happen, though a torpedo boat centre was set up there during the war. Today Osea Island is an exclusive Island offering a variety of accommodation for holidays as well as corporate and private events.

Breeding species of Essex birds include avocet, lapwing, redshank, shoveler, pochard, and bearded tit. During migration, wheatears, whinchats, marsh harriers and waders such as godwits, whimbrels, and stints can be seen.

During the winter months, the saltmarshes and mud flats of the Blackwater hosts huge flocks of wading birds and wild fowl including Avocets, Dunlin & Oyster Catchers; Brent Geese, Widgeon, Shell Duck, Teal and many less common species as well as a chance of Raptors.

The Essex Fishing Smack

Fishing Smack moored at Maldon - Painting by Doug Carpenter

The sailing smacks of Essex evolved through many centuries and their exact origins are long ago forgotten. They were built, owned and fished from the ports on the rivers Colne, Blackwater, Crouch and Roach, with others from Harwich and Leigh on Sea.

The Essex Smack is a cutter-rigged fishing vessel having various forms and configurations for different fisheries. There were three principal types in the nineteenth and early twentieth centuries. Small smacks, up to about 35 feet and about 12 tons' register, were mainly used for estuary dredging and trawling. Some 12 to 18 tones, up to about 50 feet, were used for this work at times, but were mainly fishing around the coast for sprat plus oyster dredging, five-finger starfish and sometimes mussels.

Line of fishing Smacks at Maldon Promenade 1930s

Largest of all were the seagoing smacks up to about 65 feet in length and 20 tons' register, which were mainly owned in the River Colne and at Burnham, the Colne boats fishing far afield. All were renowned for their windward ability, seaworthiness and speed.

Rowhedge and Wivenhoe villages on the Colne estuary, were pioneers in the nineteenth century. The shipyards of Sainty, Harris and Harvey succeeded in producing some of the finest smacks and yachts in the country. The smacks fishermen ventured far afield in search of oysters, and as their skill and daring gained recognition. They were in demand as skippers and crews of some of the grandest craft in the age of the big yachts. This earned them the money which in turn went into even greater and faster smacks.

Brightlingsea having deep water at the mouth of the estuary, soon joined in and throughout the second half of the century. Aldous's yard became the biggest of all the Essex smack builders, turning out thirty-six big cutters of over twenty tons between 1857 and 1867. Aldous's yard often turned out small smacks for around one hundred pounds and would trust the new owner to pay them back over a few years as they earned money from fishing.

Boat at Lea on Sea

Maldon Salt Company

Sea Salt (favoured by famous chefs) is still harvested from the Blackwater. At least 2,000 years ago, seawater was being partially evaporated and then heated in clay pots over open fires. When the water had gone, the pots were broken open to reveal the precious result: salt. Flat tide-washed marshes and low rainfall mean high salinity and the ideal place to start the Maldon Salt Company in 1882.

By 1900 orders for Maldon Salt arrive at Harrods and Fortnum and Mason, London's top food stores. The talk is good: "We found the salt much better than ordinary salt for pickling beef, a much smaller quantity being required for brine. Also gives the beef a much better flavour." declared Harrods bosses.

1955 The salt is shipped to Sweden, though more by chance than design. A local girl gives her Swedish pen-friend a basket of local Maldon salt on an exchange visit. Her father happens to be the buyer for the Co-operative food halls throughout Sweden.

2000 Delia Smith recommends Maldon Salt in her latest cookery book.

2006 Still operating from the same salt pans at their original site, Maldon Salt Company choose to go back to some very old roots with a salt works on one of the original Essex salt making sites from Saxon times.

2010 Her Majesty the Queen. visits it makes for a great day; a chance to explain the process and for everyone at Maldon to take pride in a product they know will be used by the Royal Household.

Cooks Boat Yard

Maldon, Hythe Quay Cooks Boat Yard

Walter Cook and Sons yard closed in 1992 but others now carry on the work and there are still a number of craft being restored at The Hythe; under repair and restoration including George Smeed plus a tug boat at the time of writing.

Maldon is the major berth for the charter barge fleet of Hydrogen, Thistle, Reminder and Repertor, managed by Topsail Charters who operate Glemway as a Maritime Heritage Centre. Also based on the Hythe are the East Coast Sail Trust, school ship Thalatta; the Cirdan Trust's Xylonite and the Thames Barge Sailing Club barges; Pudge, Centaur and the lighter Sailorman. Privately owned craft include Nellie, and Lady Jean. Making Maldon the main base for the barge fleet on the East Coast.

With over 60 miles of coastline, Maldon retains a extraordinary character forged over the centuries by the Districts three rivers and the North Sea. The town's links with the River Chelmer and Blackwater Estuary remain important, and Thames sailing barges can still be seen at the quayside or heading towards Heybridge Basin.

Maldon's Hythe Quay is home to the largest collection of those barges, you often see them being restored by the quayside or on blocks by the quayside having its hull maintained. This is where some of Maldon's barges were originally constructed.

The view of Hythe Quay is vastly changed to that of a one hundred years ago, along with the workers who unloaded the cargoes in the barges for transportation to Chelmsford - alas now replaced by visitors enjoying the views or partaking of refreshment at one of the two pubs about the quayside.

To access the river from Maldon Town - go down Market Hill next to the ancient library, the hill lined with many timber framed buildings including the old workhouse, leads steeply down to Fullbridge crossing over the River Chelmer. This area was once a thriving port with its wharves busy unloading ships laden with timber and other materials. It is also the home of Maldon's old railway station building which has survived despite the railway being closed by Lord Beecham in 1964. There is also limited parking by the quayside, plus plenty of spaces in the Prom car park.

The Chelmer and Blackwater Navigation
Heybridge Basin

The Lock Heybridge Basin The 'Old Ship' Inn by the quay

Today Heybridge Basin is an oasis for pleasure craft of all ages and sizes as well as being the starting point for walks along the sea wall to Maldon and beyond.

The two pubs that once served to quench the thirst of the basin workers and visiting sailors now cater for the tourists visiting this picturesque area. There is also a tea room and art and craft gallery on the sea wall. The Rivers Chelmer and Blackwater both rise in and flow through the county of Essex. The River Chelmer rises near Thaxted and towards Chelmsford, where it is joined by the River Can. It meets the River Blackwater at Langford near Maldon. The Basin at Heybridge was dug out at the sea end of the navigation to allow lighters to enter the canal via the sea lock for the unloading of their cargo's for transportation inland. The expanse of canal between the Basin and Beeleigh was cut out by hand to bypass Maldon because the town opposed the building of the canal fearing loss of trade.

Construction of the 13-mile canal to Chelmsford started about 1793 under the direction of John Rennie. The Chelmer & Blackwater has remained open and privately run throughout its history. Never having been nationalised, it continued to carry commercial freight until 1972, and an increasing number of leisure users since that time. Most of John Rennie original structures are intact, together with the entire length of the original waterway.

The River Blackwater rises in north west of Essex as the River Pant. It flows through Braintree and is joined by the River Brain before flowing towards Maldon and out to the North Sea via Heybridge Basin or the tidal river Chelmer.

Prior to the actual construction of the navigation, there had been almost 120 years of proposals for such a canal, and opposition from the port of Maldon, which anticipated that its revenues would fall if vessels could travel to Chelmsford, Essex.

Heybridge Basin is the beginning of the Chelmer & Blackwater Navigation to which it owes its creation. It was here that the Colliers' barges unloaded for the journey inland.

8 Tollesbury

The village of Tollesbury is situated on the Essex coast at the mouth of the River Blackwater, 9 miles east of the historic port of Maldon and 12 miles south of Colchester, 50 miles from London, yet it is very quiet and totally isolated. Walk out on to the sea wall and you are in another world of sparkling water, soaring sea birds and broad vistas.

Because of its geographical situation Tollesbury has for centuries, relied on the harvests from both the land and the sea and the village has become known as 'The Village of the Plough and Sail'.

Tollesbury Sail Lofts

A lovely group of buildings now preserved and in great use for tourist trade. Grade II rated and date listed 25 January 1974. Tollesbury Sail Lofts were built around the turn of the century to serve the local fishing fleet and probably the great J-Class yachts which were owned by wealthy Edwardian's and skippered around the Mediterranean by men from Tollesbury. The most well-known of these yachts was entered by Tommy Sopwith in the Americas Cup. Sopwith challenged the Americas Cup with the Endearour in 1934, and Endeavour II in 1937. He was inducted into the Americas Cup Hall of Fame in 1995.

Fellowship Afloat Charitable Trust

Trinity, Fellowship Afloat Centre at Tollesbury. Converted from a light-vessel in 1990, accommodating up to 36 guests, with the historic Estelle sailing ship in the foreground.

FACT is Fellowship Afloat Charitable Trust, a unique place for adventure, relaxation and exploring the environment. Based on a converted light vessel moored on the coast, it is an ideal activity venue for youth clubs, schools, churches, special needs groups and those wishing to gain sailing qualifications. Guests are served by the centre staff and expert volunteers who form the lively Christian community which is Fellowship Afloat.

Trinity is moored in Woodrolfe Creek, a sheltered inlet on the north side of the River Blackwater estuary.

Fellowship Afloat Charitable Trust

Tollesbury village sign

Situated on West Street The 'Sail' side of the sign shows the weather boarded sail lofts. The centre of the sign shows the yacht 'Endeavour II' which was the 1937 British challenger for the America's Cup, while on the left is painted the fishing smack 'Sallie'. Oysters and fish the harvests from the Blackwater, are shown on the supports.

On the 'Plough' side of the carved village sign, the ploughman and his team of horses are depicted working the land, Horse and plough near the water's edge. Featured on the right of the sign are fishing smacks on the River Blackwater. The village church can be seen on the top left side of the sign. A mallard and a hare are pictured on the supports.

Tollesbury Wick Nature Reserve

Tollesbury Wick Marshes

This 600-acre site is a rare example of an Essex fresh water grazing marsh, worked for decades by traditional methods sympathetic to wildlife. You should be able to see Marsh Harriers at most times of the year. The whole area is designated a Site of Special Scientific Interest, in particular because of its overwintering birds. It became an Essex Wildlife Trust reserve in 1993.

A public footpath follows the sea wall from Tollesbury Marina round the sea wall and back through the village. On this 5.5 mile walk you can appreciate the Essex coast, the history which formed it and the wildlife activity. The route is exposed to the elements so you'll need your wellies and a scarf. On your way round you'll encounter the wondrous names Woodrolfe Creek, The Leaving Head, Shinglehead Point, Big Fleet, Blockhouse Bay, Tollesbury Pier and Mill Creek.

Along the sea wall to the Leavings: There is some fringing reed and scrub development along the borrowdyke just inside the reserve which is always worth a look and a listen in summer for reed warblers and reed buntings as well as spot the dragonflies. Two hundred metres further on is the only outflow sluice for the whole marsh. Little terns are often seen searching for ten-spine sticklebacks, which thrive in the salty borrowdyke along with many insects, prawns and often some big eels.

The folding, that flat land between borrowdyke and sea wall, is good in Summer for plants like grass vetchling and spiny restharrow, and for grasshoppers and crickets, notably Roesel's bush cricket, with its persistent free-wheeling song. Regain the public footpath on the sea wall to keep a watch on the saltmarsh, which is purple with sea lavender in summer, and the muddy creeks which hold a good range of birds.

Tollesbury Wick Walk

This walk is absolutely characterful. On the seaward side you have the bustling and delightful Tollesbury Marina, plenty of sailing boats of all shapes and sizes, and views across the river to the marinas of West Mersea and St Lawrence. Set against these is a thin strip of saltmarsh, and the river itself, which at some times during the year is abundant with wild birds over wintering on the marshes.

On the landward side you have the borrowdyke winding along beside you criss-crossing the salt marshes. And finally, there are points of industrial or architectural interest, such as old WW2 buildings, views of Bradwell Power Station, the Red Hills, and the remains of the old railway line.

Over it all is the panoramic vista of the beautiful coloured Essex skies. And as you go back to the village square there are some impressive views across the river.

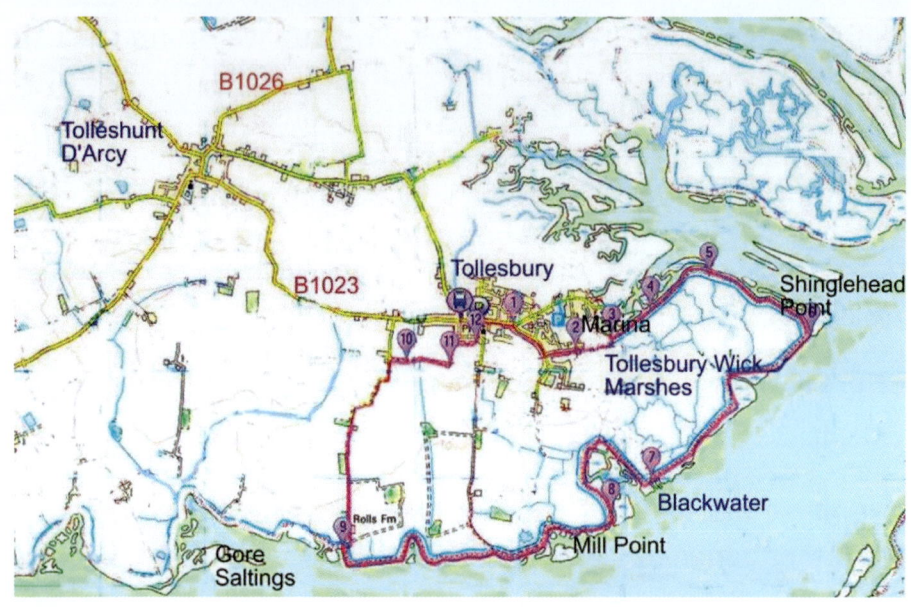

Directions
From the parking, turn right on East Street
At the fork in the road, turn right into Mell Road (1)
After 400 yards, turn left into Woodrolfe Farm lane. After a short distance the road becomes a footpath (2) continue along it until you come to the Marina.
At the Marina, turn right onto the sea wall (3).
Continue on the sea wall, past the lightship, (4) and into the nature reserve.
Continue along the sea wall - there's no need for directions here, just keep going! (5)
Distance: about 9 miles - Time taken: about 4 hours
Location: 9 miles East of Maldon - Grid Ref.: TL 956 104
Parking: Outside the King's Head, in the village square, CM9 8QU
Bus: bus Bus 91 - Witham, 92 - Colchester, 95 – Maldon 9 miles
Refreshment: The King's Head in Tollesbury and a friendly small cafe along the main road. Plus more at Tollesbury Sail Lofts.

Tollesbury Railway 1903

Tollesbury was served by a railway. This was at the end of a branch line off the main route to the Essex Coast from London's Liverpool Street station.

The Crab and Winkle Line, Tollesbury Station

The route from Kelvedon to the Tollesbury terminus is of interest to the real train enthusiast, 'Crab and Winkle' as the line was affectionately named. At the time of the passing of the Light Railways Act in 1896, the part of Essex around Tollesbury was still very remote. They were days when in many areas the railways reigned supreme, and the mooted railway from Kelvedon to Tollesbury was anticipated to enable the region to share in the benefits afforded by the age of the steam locomotive.

On the 1st October 1903 one hundred and twenty guests made the first run to Tollesbury, the train leaving its Kelvedon terminus at about 11.00am and, on its arrival at Tollesbury, 8 miles to the south east, was greeted by an enthusiastic crowd of sightseers. Guests walked the route from Tollesbury station down to the River Blackwater, following the course of the half-finished extension to Tollesbury Pier.

The extension to the pier remained open for less than 20 years and skirted the village before dropping steadily to the Blackwater. Two roads, Woodrolfe Road and Woodrolfe Farm Lane were crossed by this final section of the line. Regrettably the former did not take place and the branch line closed in 1951.

Tollesbury St. Mary's Church

The church stands at the highest part of the village. The lower part is Norman and the brick part is Tudor. The tower of the church is a most imposing structure and it may well be that here was a place of refuge for parishioners in time of attack from marauders crossing the North Sea. The lowest stage of the tower dates from the 11th Century and consists of rubble, flint and conglomerate walling with freestone quoins. The doorway is typical of the Tudor period. Above this stage are two more windows with 15th Century brickwork. The largest window in the tower is in the perpendicular style and the highest windows of brick were shaped in Tudor times. The tower is capped by parapet walls and pinnacles dating from the 17th Century. Buttresses are made from flint and brick.

There are window lights that depicted four of the famous yachts that have contended for the 'The Americas Cup', the premier yachting trophy. Yachtsmen from the Colne and Blackwater districts have been closely connected with it since the first race in 1851.

Tollesbury men enter in fifteen of the sixteen British contenders until 'Endeavour II'; the last 'Shamrock' and the two 'Endeavour' yachts were skippered by Captain Ted Heard of Tollesbury. Top left window is the schooner 'America' which first won the historic race around the Isle of Wight. Second from the top is the schooner 'Cambria' which contended in 1870; third from top is 'Shamrock II' the challenger in 1899; and bottom is 'Endeavour I'. In the right hand light are to be seen the coastal vessels that plied the Essex waters. Top right is a Billy Boy; second from the top a ketch rigged barge; third is a Thames barge, especially built to carry straw and hay for the stables and horses of London; and bottom right is a Tollesbury oyster smack showing the rig of about 1922.

St Marys Church interior

9 Burnham on Crouch

The Royal Corinthian Yacht Club – Digital Art

Burnham-on-Crouch is a town in the Maldon District of Essex. It lies on the north bank of the River Crouch. It is Essex's "Cowes of the East", a leading place to go yachting, a historic town on the East Coast of England, first as a ferry port, later as a fishing port known for its oyster beds.

Hosting the internationally famous 'Burnham Week' started as a series of contests in the late 1800's between the London Sailing Club and The Royal Corinthian Yacht Club. As The Royal Burnham Yacht Club and the Crouch Yacht Club opened the contests expanded into a more organised week of sailing. Competition takes place in such classes as Class 1 to 6, Hunter 707, Dragons, Squibs, Sandhoppers, Osprey, Phantom and Laser. Racing is best watched from the water, you can hire a boat or maybe use your own. Some of the races start and finish off the Quay and take place on the River Crouch although some start to the east of Burnham travelling out to sea. Go along the sea wall will allow good views of the racing.

The host yacht Clubs are; Royal Burnham Yacht Club, Royal Corinthian Yacht Club, Crouch Yacht Club and Burnham Sailing Club all host dinners and entertainments during the evenings.

RCYC in Burnham-on-Crouch

Burnham-on-Crouch is the Capital of the picturesque Dengie Hundred much of which is unchanged since its listing in the Doomsday Book. Here there is many other attractions such as fossil laden cliffs to a working steam railway museum. Nestling in the rural Essex countryside on a farm near Burnham on Crouch, the Mangapps Railway Museum is a privately owned working museum with locomotives, rolling stock, restored buildings and memorabilia gathered from all over East Anglia.

Mangapps Railway – Digital Art

Burnham Ferry between Wallasea Island and Burnham-on-Crouch Marina

The Ferry runs 6 days a week excluding Wednesdays from Easter Friday to the end of September. The road trip from Burnham to Wallasea Island by car takes approximately an hour; the ferry crosses the river in around ten minutes.

The ferry is accessible for foot passengers and cyclists alike to cross the River Crouch to enjoy the restaurants, bars, gift shops and cafés Burnham has to offer as well as beautiful riverside walks and miles of cycling along the marsh paths. The boat, a Searover 18 is fully Maritime and Coastguard Agency approved and is used by numerous other ferry and commercial operators.

The Crouch, whose estuary is the base of many oyster fisheries. The beacons out at sea tell the tale of danger, and point to the dreaded Maplin sands, and the treacherous shoals that culminate in the fatal Goodwins. At Foulness the tenants of Lord Winchilsea have most successfully reclaimed a space of menacing foreshore from the sea, but as a rule these expanses yield little better than coarse marsh grass, wild fowl, and expanses of salt marsh, the island of Foulness, which is formed by the curvature of one of the smaller channels, half river and half creek, which are abundant around the islands, is the oasis of this marshy desert.

Birdwatchers, nature lovers, walkers and cyclists will be attracted to Wallasea Island where the RSPB is developing the Wallasea Wetland Project, the largest nature reserve of its kind in Europe.

At high water the Crouch estuary is a pleasant enough arm of the sea, and as the river was navigable for brigs of respectable tonnage at Burnham in old times, and for smaller craft to Fainbridge Ferry, the ruddy and white barges impart a refreshing animation to the scene. Particularly is this the case when the little fleet of oyster boats are on active service. The River Crouch rises from two springs in Little Bursted and Langdon, the district lying between the high and picturesque uplands of these parts, Billericay and Langdon Hill. A small stream for a while, the Crouch passes several villages, the branches joining forces at Kamsden Grays; it becomes navigable for barges at Battlesbridge, and for sea-going brigs and schooners at Hullbridge, in which place the scenery is pretty and undulating.

Burnham Yacht Harbour and Marina

The harbour surrounded by the beautiful unspoilt Dengie Marshes is an oasis for many visiting wildfowl. From here it is a short distance to the open waters of the Thames Estuary and the peaceful backwaters of the Rivers Alde, Deben, Orwell, Stour and Thames. The yacht harbour in Burnham on Crouch has been a major feature of this well-known sailing town since its construction in 1989. Yachting became fashionable in the late 1800's and the Royal Corinthian Yacht Club and London Sailing Clubs opened in1892. The boating activity led to the development of boat building, sail makers and other related business which took place around the river front.   The commencement of 'Burnham Week' brought Burnham to national importance as a yachting centre. Burnham on Crouch has been the base for a lifeboat since 1966 when the inshore lifeboat station was established with a D class inshore lifeboat behind the Royal Corinthian Yacht Club.

The inshore rescue boat was then launched via a trailer and the yacht club ramp. In 2002 Burnham RNLI opened a new floating boathouse which is one of only three in the UK.

Bridgemarsh Island is on the river Crouch. This island's old river wall is a thin, broken strip of eroding Kentish rag stone, topped with mud and grass, long-since breached. It was abandoned in the 1930s, the final occupants – the Gooches, lived in the upper rooms of their lonely farmhouse as the tides washed through the ground floor twice a day. The island in the 1950s was alive with sheep and cattle, the dykes and flats home to vast numbers of eel and duck. At the west end was still the old farmhouse, by that time ruined and empty. But then the seawall was breached again and all the livestock drowned. This Islands has a unique character, a location very different to the surrounding coast.

Groynes in Bridgemarsh Creek and Bridgemarsh Island

Burnham on Sea Marshland

The marshland of the estuary begins to assert itself around Essex, and Burnham is to all intents and purposes the seaport of this portion of the Hundreds a local term applying to the levels between the Crouch and the Colne known as the Dengie Hundreds.

All around the Dengie peninsular are nature reserves and footpaths on or adjacent to trail member's farms. These allow unrivalled access to the countryside and wildlife habitats. The estuaries in the Hundreds are internationally recognised for their wildlife. Many opportunities exist for bird watchers, artists and walkers to explore the coast and countryside via an extensive network of footpaths.

R.A.F. Bradwell Bay Memorial

RAF Bradwell Bay is a former Royal Air Force station located 9.5 miles east of Maldon, Essex, England and 3.1 miles south west of West Mersea, Essex. The airfield was first used as grass landing strip for the nearby firing ranges before being turned into a RAF station with concrete runways and hangars. The station is unique as it was the only fighter station where the Fog Investigation and Dispersal Operation was used.

Part of the site is currently being used by the Bradwell nuclear power station. Agricultural buildings, built in the '70s and '80s on runways one and two. Bradwell nuclear power station is a partially decommissioned Magnox power station located on the Dengie peninsula at the mouth of the River Blackwater, Essex.

As of 2016, China General Nuclear Power Group and China National Nuclear Corporation are considering Bradwell for the site of a new nuclear power station.

Fambridge to Burnham Walk

This scenic placid riverside walk can be started or finished by train. The Crouch Estuary is an oasis for bird life and heaven for boating enthusiasts. There are outstanding views of unspoilt land either side of the estuary, troubled only by the cry of sea birds and the occasional hum of a distant train passing along the valley floor.

Starting at North Fambridge Railway Station, the walk goes past the Owl Cam at Blue House Farm, and onto the sea wall by Fambridge Marina. If a 5-mile walk is your limit you can divert at Althorne Marina to Althorne Train Station, also on the Southminster Line. From Althorne, the path proceeds on the sea wall with views of wading birds and the changing landscape of the Crouch estuary. The terrain is flat apart from a small section inland at "The Cliff" and Creeksea. After walking around the Burnham Yacht Harbour, the walk ends on The Quay where there is a selection of fine dining places.

Distance: 10½ miles
Time taken: 4 hours
Location: North Fambridge, nr Burnham-on-Crouch, CM3 6NP
Grid Ref.: TQ 857 978
Parking: NCP at Station, CM3 6NP
Train: Wickford - Southminster
Refreshment: North Fambridge: Ferry Boat Inn, Althorne: Three Horseshoes (CM3 6DP)
Burnham on Crouch: The Anchor Hotel, The Star Inn, Cabin Dairy Tearooms
Directions

Go North to Fambridge railway station and head south towards Fambridge Road. Continue south for a quarter of a mile and take the gravel path which forks left from the bend in the road.

Check out the Owl Cam at Blue House Farm, before taking the gate to its right. Follow the field edge path for 230 yards to a field gate, and head south to the steps up on to the seawall. On the seawall, turn left and head east. After about a mile and a half the path heads north east around Bridgemarsh Island, another Site of Special Scientific Interest.

Eventually you come to some signs of human habitation, which is Althorne. If you want to return via Althorne train station, which is a third of a mile north of the Creek, turn left at the marina, up the track past 'Papillon'.

Go on towards Burnham on Crouch. After a quarter of a mile, the path turns north around an inlet. At the end of the inlet, a gate to the right enables you to go along the side of the estuary.

Carry on walking by the river. After two-thirds of a mile, the path heads inland and ascends the Cliff. As you descend, you will see a gap between the hedge line by a small jetty, where you can pick up the seawall path again.

Two thirds of a mile after this, the path again heads inland, where you turn left down some steps to a gate. Pass along the field edge heading east. Exit the field through a gate, and turn right on a track towards the marina. Carry on east along the coastal footpath.

Go inland through Burnham Yacht Harbour and return to the river walk into Burnham on Crouch. From there, tea rooms by the War Memorial and pubs are available on or near The Quay. The train station on the High Street and walking north west to join Station Road. The station is approximately three-quarters of a mile from The Quay.

Bradwell on Sea

Bradwell Power Station looking across Mersea to Dengie

Bradwell Power Station is close to the Essex coastline. Electricity generation started at the nuclear power station in 1962 and ceased in 2002. During its lifetime the site generated nearly 60 TWh of electricity. The site is following an accelerated decommissioning programme and is now more than halfway through a programme of work which should see it become the first reactor site in the UK to enter Care and Maintenance preparations in 2015.

Bradwell Waterside is a small marina hamlet near the power station. It is located about 9 km (5.6 miles) north-northeast of Southminster in the Dengie Hundreds. Southminster lies at the centre of the Dengie One Hundred peninsula which was a region of marsh and wealthy farmland and until the growth of Burnham on Crouch was the bigger settlement in times gone by.

Bradwell Shell Bank Nature Reserve – Digital Art

Bradwell on Sea Walk

Although this is a long walk, it's not demanding. The terrain is level, and the footpaths are well maintained. About half the route follows the coastal path, which is picturesque, with a variety of visual interest.

From the mudflats and seascape, to the ancient Chapel of St Peter-on-the-Wall, the sandy beaches along the northern shore, Bradwell marina with dozens of boats bobbing around on the water, even the visually bold power station: there's always plenty to see and enjoy. You don't really need directions for this part of the walk. The first section, going east from the car park to the seashore, and the last section taking you back to Tillingham (a really pretty village; try the The Fox and Hounds for lunch) however, over fields and through woods, does warrant some guidance.

Distance: 12 Miles

Time taken: 4½ Hours

Location:9 miles east of Maldon

OS Explorer Map: 176

Grid Ref.: TL 992 038

Parking: West Field car park, Tillingham, opp. St. Nicholas Church, CM0 7TW

Bus: Bus D1, two hourly from Maldon, no Sunday service

Refreshment: The Green Man, Bradwell Waterside

The Fox and Hounds, Tillingham which has great fresh food and a very warm welcome.

Burnham on Crouch water front

The Chapel St. Peter Ad Murum - Digital Art

St Cedd, an Irish Missionary, landed at Bradwell in AD 654 and established the Church of St Peters on the inner wall of the Roman fortress. England's oldest chapel is there to be visited but only the earthworks of the Roman fort remain.

The Chapel of

St PETER AD MURUM

BUILT ON THE WALL OF
THE ROMAN FORT "OTHONA"
BY ST. CEDD, 654A.D.

"In this place the word is revealed to you"

**SERVICES: SUNDAY EVENINGS JULY - AUGUST, 6.30PM
FOR DETAILS, SEE NOTICE BOARDS OR
www.bradwellchapel.org**

CHAPLAINS: BRADWELL RECTORY, Tel. 01621 776203

An ecumenical pilgrimage is held here on the 1st Saturday in July each year

"Bringing the people of Essex together"

The tiny chapel of St Peter-on-the-Wall, at Bradwell-on-Sea on Essex's Dengie peninsula. The mini-pilgrimage feels appropriate – the tiny church, and is one of the oldest and most atmospheric places of worship in the UK and deserves a little reverence.

Dengie Peninsula

The Dengie Peninsula is an area of South Essex, bounded by the River Blackwater to the north, the River Crouch to the south and the North Sea to the east. The western boundary of the old "Dengie Hundred" ran from North Fambridge to Woodham Walter: The nearby town of Maldon was not part of the Dengie Hundred as it was a borough in its own right. The area has a relatively low population density, with large areas of farm and marsh land, the largest town is Burnham on Crouch.

The Villages of Dengie

The Dengie Hundred has been the home to man since iron age when he discovered the rich soil and the mild coastal climate. The Romans arrived and built forts and homes, they were followed by the Saxons who gave the area its name.

Steeple parish where a small Christian Cluniac priory was founded in the twelfth century as a cell to the establishment at Lewes. This priory was dissolved in 1525, and the buildings have long since disappear.

Creeksea village, on the Dengie peninsula to the north side of the River Crouch, one mile west of Burnham on Crouch and it is part of the Maldon district. Creeksea Sailing Club founded in 1957 has launching facilities on the River Crouch.

Althorne is a village on the Crouch, adjacent to, and combined ecclesiastically with, Cricksea. The church of St. Andrew is an interesting building of flint and stone, mostly in the Perpendicular style, but with a modern brick chancel. Part of the rood-stair remains; and the curious brasses to Margaret Hyklott (1502) and William Hyklott (1508) who "paid for the workmanship of the walls of this Church."

St Lawrence is a small riverside Essex village between Steeple and Bradwell on Sea. The village is rural with a population centred around Main Road and St Lawrence Drive. The church St. Lawrence stands on an eminence overlooking the village, where it was rebuilt of Kentish rag stone in a perpendicular style in 1877-8. Southminster is a large parish, with a prosperous village, on the Dengie peninsula formed between the river Crouch and Blackwater. The church of St. Leonard is a fine cruciform building, consisting of chancel, transepts, nave, north porch, and a lofty embattled west tower containing six bells. Traces of Norman work appear in the plain south doorway and elsewhere; but there are clear signs of reconstruction in the walls.

Tillingham's church of St. Nicholas is from Norman origin, as shown by the north doorway and structure of the walls; but the predominant styles are Early English and Perpendicular

Popular beaches on the Dengie peninsula are: Steeple Bay Holiday Site, St Lawrence Centre shingle beach, Bradwell on Sea has Othona and Down Hall beaches is mostly sand and shingle.

Dengie Sunken barges used as a Breakwaters

Dengie nature reserve is a 3,105 hectare biological and geological Site of Special Scientific Interest between the estuaries of the Blackwater and Crouch near Bradwell-on-Sea in Essex. It is also a National Nature Reserve, a Special Protection Area, a Nature Conservation Review site, a Geological Conservation Review site and a Ramsar site. It is part of the Essex estuaries Special Area of Conservation. An area of 12 hectares is the Bradwell Shell Bank nature reserve, which is managed by the Essex Wildlife Trust. It consists of large, remote area of tidal mud-flats and salt marshes at the eastern end of the Dengie peninsula.

10 Southend-on-Sea

The largest destination on the Essex Coast is Southend-on-Sea stretching about seven miles of mainly sandy beaches. Originally the "south end" of the ancient village of Prittlewell. which is the ecclesiastical mother of Southend, consists principally of two streets, at right angles to each other, on the side of a hill overlooking the Thames. The mansion called " The Priory " stands on the site, and includes a few relics of the Cluniac monastery founded by Robert of Essex, son of Sweyn. The founder gave to the community the church of Prittlewell, with its two chapels of Sutton and Eastwood, and the tithes of the hamlet at Milton, an arrangement which was disturbed at the Dissolution of 1536. The church of St. Mary is a stately building of Kentish rag stone, mainly of fifteenth-century date, consisting of chancel with south chapel, nave with south aisle, and west tower, now containing a ring of ten bells. From the Domesday Survey it appears that there was a church here before the Conquest, though it would seem to have been considerably enlarged soon after that event.

Southend was originally home to a few poor fisherman huts and farms that lay at the southern extremity of Prittlewell Priory land. In the 1790s landowner Daniel Scratton sold off land either side of what become the High Street, and the Royal Hotel and the Royal Terrace were completed by 1794. Southend-on-Sea become a popular summer resort around the early 1800s.

Southend Pier - looking towards Kent

The sandy Three Shells is Southend's most central beach, offering easy access to Adventure Island, the pier, the splendid shopping centre and pedestrianize High Street, as well as cafés, pubs on the seafront and a large amusement area.

Southend is on the north side of the Thames estuary only 40 miles east of central London.

The pier is the longest in this world at over one-mile-long - indeed 1.33 miles. Like the Eiffel Tower is to Paris, or the Empire State Building to New York, then Southend Pier is to Essex. The pier was started in 1828 and completed in 1830 and with its Electric train to take you to the end of the pier, as if going over the mud flats it was like the thrill of a luxury holiday. The electric tramway opened in 1890 with 1 car operating on 0.75 miles of single track. The following year the track had been extended to the full 1.25 miles and more cars were added until four trains were in use. In 1949 the rolling stock was replaced with four new trains similar in design to the London Underground stock. Between 1984 and 1986 the Pier was repaired and a new track laid and two new trains commenced operation. The pier is a true survival story, having been beset by fires; a fire in 1995 destroyed the bowling alley at the start of the pier and another fire in October 2005 damaged the far end of the pier.

The trains leave the pier head every quarter to and quarter past the hour until 15 minutes before closing. At peak times a two train service is operated. Trains leave both ends at a quarter past, half past, a quarter to, and on the hour. Going on Southend Pier or the train is not free. If you need a wheelchair, you can hire one from the Visitor Information Centre by calling them in advance on 01702 618747.

Southend on Sea pier at night

Southend on Sea Pier around 1886

You can fish by licence fee off the pier were you may land mackerel, plaice or flounder, you have a choice of the fishing positions: Stem or the Pier Head. The cafe at the end of the pier has been used by Jamie Oliver for his series Jimmy and Jamie's Friday Food Night.

At Southend-on-Sea you'll find all the traditional seaside pleasures along the seven glorious miles of seafront. Thrill-seekers rejoice with the vast range of water sports, at the Marine Activities Centre – ride the roller-coasters at Adventure Island or discover a world of watery wonder at the Sea-Life Adventure Aquarium.

Southend-on-Sea has great and varied shopping facilities. The Town Centre is a unique shopping destination with a variety of quirky independent boutiques and 'big name' high street stores, and with over three hundred mouth-watering places to eat and a dazzling live music and nightlife scene, you really are spoilt for choice.

On the Cliff Lift you can take a journey on an iconic feature of Southend's rich heritage with grand views of the Pier and estuary. The lift can hold up to 18 people and has a ramp for disabled access and pushchairs. The Cliff Lift runs between Western Esplanade and Clifton Terrace, where you will find The Royals shopping centre within a short walking distance along the promenade.

The Royal Pavilion can be found at the entrance to Southend pier, and it's a grand venue for performances of any kind, and hosts flourishing Jazz and Comedy Festivals. Perched on the cliffs in Westcliff, the Cliff's Pavilion has hosted some top name musicians, comedians, plays and the great British traditional pantomimes every year, and remains an intrinsic part of Southend's culture.

Boats at Marine Parade Beach, Southend-on-Sea c.1955

Southend historic cliff lift reopens following refurbishment. The funicular cliff lift was first opened on August Bank Holiday 1912, ninety-eight years after it first went into service, Southend's cliff lift is set to carry passengers once more.

The Georgian structure will allow visitors to travel between the seafront and the Clifftown Conservation Area.

The £650,000 refurbishment included the removal of the lift carriage which was then completely refurbished. Work was also carried out on the track the carriage operates on. The original single car could take up to 30 people at a time

"The stations were refurbished earlier as part of the Heritage Lottery fund granted to the Cliff garden area.

During the summer season the lift will operate daily between 10am and 5.45pm. Each trip will cost 50p.

The Cliffs Pavilion, Southend

The Cliffs Pavilion is the largest purpose-built performing arts venue in Essex and presents in excess of 300 performances each year across a wide range of live entertainment from ballet, opera and classical music, through to top-name comedians and singers, to West End musicals, stand-up rock concerts and the largest pantomime in the South East.

Station Road, Southend-on-Sea SS0 7QD Phone: 01702 390657

Palace Theatre opened in 1912, this delightful Edwardian Theatre retains all of the charm of its music hall origins including the sweeping grand staircase to the Circle, alongside many original features such as the regency-style domes on the boxes and the ornately-decorated billboard frames on the proscenium arch.

Palace Theatre, 430 London Road, Southend on Sea, SS0 9LA

The Kursaal, Southend on Sea

The Kursaal was the world's first ever theme park, pre-dating Coney Island in America. Designed by the architect Campbell Sherrin, also responsible for amongst other things, the Brompton Oratory, the Kursaal building and its Dome were at the cutting edge of architectural design.

The Kursaal included a circus, ballroom, arcade with amusements, dining hall and billiard room. There were many firsts at the Kursaal. The world's first lady lion tamer, the world's first lady wall of death rider performed here, it was the first venue in England for the display of Al Capone's personal car from Chicago, and Eric the sixty ton stuffed whale!

Southend was the nearest seaside resort to London. Following Sir John Lubbock's Bank Holiday Act of 1871, the first Monday in August became a national holiday, and the London, Tilbury and Southend Railway Company posted bills on hoardings all over London advertising Southend as the capital's nearest resort.

After falling into disrepair the opinion of Southend Council was that the Kursaal had become a 'tatty Victorian antiquated fairground'. In January 1974 the owners of the fairground rides were given notice to quit, and requested to remove their rides at the earliest opportunity. It was in this year that the biggest permanent ride in the park, the Cyclone coaster – which had operated for 37 seasons – was demolished. Outline planning permission was granted for the building of blocks of flats in the Kursaal gardens.

The Kursaal buildings were placed on the historic buildings list, and in April 1994 the dome and remaining structure were protected by the Grade II listed status by English Heritage.

In February 1998 the building was purchased by Dean and Bowes for a refit and in March 1998 the first phase of the restored Kursaal was opened to the public again.

From Southend the coast becomes low and bends somewhat to the south-east till Shoeburyness is reached. Shoeburyness, rather more than three miles from Southend, was a garrison town, and had a "School of Gunnery." Most of the big guns used in our army were tested there, and long ranges seawards had been established. A walk along the beach will bring to view targets of various thickness; and after gun-practice the shot are recovered from the sand in which they have been embedded.

Dengie Flats

The Essex coast now turns to the north-east and we pass a group of islands lying at the mouth of the Crouch. Foulness Point is the extreme point of the largest island, and Holywell Point is on the opposite coast.

From this last point to Sales Point the coast runs almost due north, and the district known as Dengie Flats is not without interest especially to bird watchers. Dengie nature reserve is a 3,105 hectare biological and geological Site of Special Scientific Interest between the estuaries of the Blackwater and Crouch near Bradwell-on-Sea. Essex has been often described, below is the account given by Mr. Rider Haggard, who visited this neighbourhood in 1901. He writes:

"The view looking over the Dengie Flats and St Peter's Sands from the summit of the earthen bank which keeps out the sea, was very desolate and strange. Behind us lay a vast, drear expanse of land won from the ocean in days' bygone, bordered on one side by the Blackwater and on the other by the Crouch Rivers, and saved, none too well, from the mastery of the waves by the sloping earthen bank on which we stood. In front, thousands of acres of grey mud where grew dull, unwholesome-looking grasses. Far, far away on this waste expanse two tiny, moving specks, men engaged in seeking for samphire or some other treasure of the ooze-mud. Then the thin, white lip of the sea, and beyond its sapphire edge in the half-distance the gaunt skeleton of a long-wrecked ship. To the north on the horizon a line of trees: to the west, over the great plain, where stood one or two lonely farms, another line of trees. On the distant deep some sails, and in the middle marsh, a barge gliding up a hidden creek as though she moved across the solid land. Then, spread like a golden garment over the vast expanses of earth and ocean, the flood of sunshine, and in our ears the rush of the north-west gale and the thrilling song of larks hanging high above the yellow, salt-soaked fields."

Shoebury near Southend-on-Sea

Shoebury East is long and sandy and backed by a large grassy area that's very popular for picnics. Located between Pig's Bay a large Ministry of Defence site, and the former Shoeburyness Artillery Barracks. The bay is in East Shoebury, a small beachhead area. The main entrance to the site is at Blackgate Road, Shoeburyness. This is also the gateway to the island of Foulness, the fourth largest island off the coast of England.

Land was first bought here for use as an artillery range in 1849, and the site is still mainly used as a weapons testing facility. Large areas of land and tidal sands allow long range testing of tank and artillery shells over distances of up to 27 kilometres. East beach is home to the Essex Kite-surfing Club.

Shoeburyness Artillery Barracks, Clock Tower, Horseshoe Barracks

Shoebury Garrison is a unique area of national importance. Its history, archaeology and historic buildings, and its incomparable setting overlooking the mouth of the Thames Estuary with adjoining beaches, parkland and nature reserves make it a interesting area to explore. Located on slightly raised land at the mouth of the Thames estuary, Shoebury has had strategic importance since prehistoric times. The Garrison is at; Hospital Road, Shoeburyness, Essex, SS3 9WB

Shoebury North is a pleasant little village has a stone-built church, mainly of thirteenth-century date, but much altered in 1885. Shoebury South has the village church of St. Andrew is a small stone building of Norman age, originally a chapel belonging to the Cluniac Priory at Prittlewell. The Norman remains appear in the chancel-arch, with wreathed mouldings, and in the rounded heading of a window. Most of the fabric is in the fifteenth century style, but an earlier squint and low-side window are preserved.

In the 6th century Saxon invaders re-established a settlement at Shoebury which later became a base for the Danes who sought to invade the Saxon kingdom. Through the medieval and post medieval periods the area remained isolated and rural.

St Mary's Church, North Shoebury

North Shoebury was once Shoebury Parva and Little Shoebury, is a district and former village in the north-east of Southend-on-Sea in the English county of Essex. The parish church stands on the West side of the parish. The walls are of ragstone-rubble with some flint; the dressings are of Reigate and other limestone; the roofs are tiled. The church was built during the course of the 13th century.

Foulness Island

Foulness is the largest of the Essex islands and the fourth largest island off the coast of England. It is located near Southend-on-Sea with its vast and lonely stretches of isolated marshland. The island's name derives from 'fulga-naess', the old English for 'wild birds nest'. Foulness and the adjoining Maplin Sands are internationally famous as a haven for wildlife. It has the second largest colony of Avocets and is a winter home for thousands of wading birds and Brent Geese.

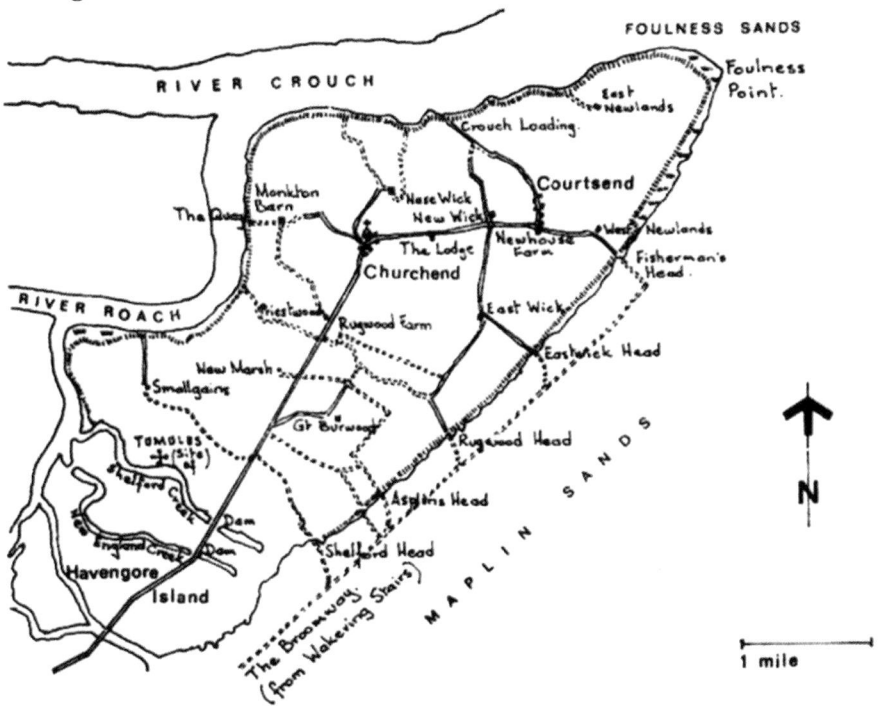

Foulness Conservation & Archaeological Society converted the former Foulness Primary School into Foulness Heritage Centre by Bob Crump. Together with many volunteers and many hours of hard work the centre opened in February 2003. It is open from 12 noon till 4pm every first Sunday of the month from April to October. The school had been empty for many years and the renovation work was carried out by volunteers with the aid of grants from 'Awards for All' and QinetiQ.

It opened in February 2003 and has received a constant stream of visitors from both the UK and abroad ever since.

Foulness Incumbents. Barling & Wakering Heritage

Seal watching trips pass by Wallasea Island & Foulness Island, always looking out for birds & waders, at the seal colony the boat drops anchor and learn about the seals and why they are there. Also cruising through the winding creeks to view the other Islands of: Potton, New England, Havengore, or Rushley. Provided by: Nature Break Wildlife Cruises.

To discover Foulness Island or walk the Broomway http://www.wildlifetrips.org.uk/

South Essex Villages

Great Wakering church of St. Nicholas is of Norman foundation, built mainly of stone and rubble, and consisted originally of chancel, nave, south porch, and west tower, to which a priest's house was added at some unknown date, and north transept in 1843. Minor alterations were made at the restorations of 1870 and 1907. The lower part of tower is unquestionably of early Norman date, but the upper part, with double light windows and square shingled spire, would appear to be fourteenth-century work. The present ring of five bells dates from 1808 only. The small building against the west face of tower has a projection on its south side, enclosing a newel staircase to the upper room. It was probably erected in fifteenth century for the accommodation of the priest serving from Beeleigh Abbey, to which the church once belonged. The chancel is supposed to have been built originally with a rounded apse, which was altered in the thirteenth century, when the lofty pointed arch and lancet windows were introduced. The modern transept is nearly square, and is thrown open to the chancel by two arches, supported on an octagonal column with moulded cap. Part of the old rood-stair remains, with other relics, but there are no monuments of importance. Little Wakering this area of this parish is actually larger than that of Great Wakering, including, as it does, the islands of " New England " and " Little Polton "; but it is very thinly populated, and, in fact, consists largely of marsh land. The church of St. Mary was restored in 1878, when a Norman window was uncovered in the chancel wall; but the fabric generally is in the fifteenth-century style.

There is an arched recess in nave, supposed to mark the site of the founder's tomb, but gives no key to his identity. The fine west tower, with shingled spire, was erected c. 1420, and contains three bells dated 1707.

Ashingdon is a village and civil parish in Essex, England. It is located about 2.5 miles north of Rochford and is 13 miles southeast from the county town of Chelmsford

South Fambridge is a village in Essex, England. It is located about 300 yards from the River Crouch. The village lies within the Rochford district and the parliamentary constituency of Rayleigh. The village once had a small airfield which no longer exists, having been converted into a residential estate named Pemberton Field after Noel Pemberton Billing. On 20 February 2009 it was the 100th anniversary of the first experimental flights beside the River Crouch meadows.

North Fambridge is on the north bank of the River Crouch opposite South Fambridge and is served by North Fambridge railway station on the Crouch Valley Line.

The Ferry Boat Inn. The North Fambridge Yacht Club is based in the village.

Holy Trinity Church has been serving the community for at least 200 years

Adjoining the village is Blue House Farm, a 605-acre. Site of Special Scientific Interest and nature reserve owned by the Essex Wildlife Trust.

Fambridge Yacht Haven is in a charming location on the River Crouch, set within the beautiful Essex countryside and surrounded by natural saltings and farmland, yet ideally positioned for easy access to and from the city of London.

The RSPB exists to conserve wild birds and the environment

Wallasea Island Wild Coast Project

Marsh Harrier Digital Art

There is a landmark conservation and engineering scheme for the 21st century, on a scale never before attempted in the UK and the largest of its type in Europe.

The Essex coast is a wild and stunning place, a haven for wildlife and a source of livelihood for local communities. Today, less than one tenth of this wild coast remains. Prior to being enclosed by the current sea walls, Wallasea 'Island' was made up of five separate saltmarsh islands. These areas of saltmarsh were progressively enclosed by sea defences, eventually developing the current island shape. Some small-scale arable areas were present periodically but the area was largely managed with sheep as coastal grazing marsh until the drainage and its conversion to arable land took place from the 1930s.

The Wild Coast Project will involve flooding a large part of Wallasea Island by eventually breaching the sea walls into the River Roach in six places creating a range of habitats for wildfowl and other marine species. The material will consist of clay, chalk and gravel and will help transform into nearly 1,500 acres of tidal wildlife habitat.

The Essex Archipelago

Here we have a group of six islands in a large body of water or onshore marshland at the southern end of Essex. A unique group separated by tidal creeks that has a beauty and wildness of its own. Four islands are owned by the MOD; Foulness, New England, Havengore and Potton Island. The other two Wallasea and Rushley are privately owned. Foulness and Wallasea Island have already been covered, the other four are:

Havengore Island is at the southern angle of the cluster of islands, is of an oval figure, bounded by the sea and the creeks adjoining with the river Broomhill. It had only 18 inhabitants, and about 810 acres of land, all extra-parochial, except Sharpness Farm, and a small portion of land, called Temple Marsh, which are in Little Wakering parish. It is the property of Lady Sparrow, and Mr. James Tabor is the only resident farmer. The new bridge links Havengore Island to New England and Foulness Islands. The name is derived from 'haven' (for fishermen) and 'gor', which is Old English for the ever-present mud. The old parish of Havengore was known in the 13th century as Havenemersche.

Rushley Island in 1781 John Harriott began to enclose the whole island with three miles of seawall. A farm and several wells were constructed. The 200-acre island cost Harriott £40 pounds to buy. In 1791 the island was flooded. Harriott abandoned his dreams and emigrated to America. The island provided evidence of Roman activity. The name of Russhleye was first recorded in 1576.

Local racehorse trainer and one-time Rushley owner, Frank Threadgold once bred a horse named after the island. Not very prosperous at racing, the horse was retired for breeding by the Threadgold families, who have farmed land at Great Wakering since the 1930s.

Potton Creek, Potton Island - Digital Art

Potton Island today it is subject to Ministry of Defence restrictions on access, and there is little to see there anyway. The island is 2 miles long and 1-mile-wide, and is the most westerly of the five islands in the Essex Archipelago – 1-mile north of Great Wakering. Access is through Great Wakering Common. The Potton name comes from a personal name 'Pott(a)'. Other names referring to it are 'Pottyng(e)' or 'Pottyngore' (1419) and 'Pottingwick' (1612). There are also other references from the 13th century. Evidence of occupation of Potton Island dates back to Neolithic, Bronze Age, and Roman times. Potton wildlife in the form of rabbits, hares, partridges, widgeon, mallard, teal, pochard, and shelduck.

New England Island Flooded in 1897 and 1953. The Island belongs to Little Wakering parish. It was the area's principal breeding grounds for sheep. During the 16th century it was in part-ownership of Lord Rich. The Ministry of Defence took over in 1915. No one lives on the Island today.

The beautifully captivating and wild New England Creek is the boundary for Foulness's close neighbours Havengore and New England Island.

The Broomway Walk

Broomway the most perilous byway in England

Broomway the notorious tidal path off the Essex coast is a public rights of way leaving the mainland of Essex at Wakering Stairs, with a causeway out to Maplin Sands, that is separated from the coast by a band of mud known as the Black Grounds for good reason. As you approach the sands the Broomway bends round to the north east, runs parallel to the coast, passes the mouth of Havengore Creek, continues to run parallel to the coast, and then crosses back over to the coast of Foulness Island, by means of a series of meandering causeways.

The origins of the Broomway are uncertain; it is a causeway across Maplin Sands, exposed at low tide, there is uncertainty if this is a natural or a man-made phenomenon, it seems to date back to Roman times. What is certain is that the churchyard on Foulness contains the graves of at least sixty people who have died trying to travel across it, for it is extremely treacherous.

The first recorded name of the Broomway was in 1419 the mysterious path connecting the mainland to Foulness Island. Residents call ditches upside down hedges; Hill House was built on the highest point of the island.

You have to get your timing right with regard to the tide, and even if you do, the water can come in fast, from several directions at once, and does not necessarily conform to the times on the tide tables; the path saunters and shifts, and several of the fateful victims have perished in quicksand. A further complication lies in the susceptibility of the area to unpredictable and quick-forming sea mists, limiting visibility to yards, and almost guaranteeing fatal disorientation. "Public Rights of way across Maplin Sands can be dangerous - seek local guidance".

Leigh on Sea

Leigh on Sea Harbour

Leigh on Sea is situated around the north bank on the Thames about 30 miles east of London. This old town features a traditional sea fishing heritage. It was described within the Doomsday book where it was named 'Legra'. From these small beginnings Leigh on sea grew into an essential port. The Mayflower is believed to docked at Leigh-on-Sea to take on provisions and passengers prior to it is epic voyage towards the new world with the Pilgrim Fathers.

Old Leigh has its own unique charm and character of a small fishing hamlet. Due to its good position on the shipping route to London, it began to grow and by the 16th century had become a prosperous port. Leigh's deep water channel silted up and the importance of the town diminished.

This charming old village boasts beautiful sunsets, a beautiful old cobbled streets and pretty clap board cottages. It is also famous for its shellfish. There's a now smaller but active fleet of cockle boats, which keep alive the reputation of Leigh global seafood trade.

The picturesque cockle sheds are property of old Leigh households who've followed this trade for generations.

The sheds are open daily, selling a wide selection of seafood which includes local specialities of which cockles, mussels, winkles are favourites and shrimps, crabs, prawns and lobsters are much enjoyed.

Due to the significant number and premium quality of practising artists inside the town, many individuals now refer to Leigh on Sea as the St. Ives of the East. Founded in 1997 by local artists, the annual Art Trail is established around this pretty estuary town. Come to this delightful fishing town to seek out the studios and shops as you discover this artistic landmarks of the East.

Leigh on Sea Sunset

Leigh Regatta in September, organised by the Lions Club of Leigh on Sea, with assistance from the Sea Scouts of Old Leigh hold the event annually. The hopeful great weather encourages a large crowd who enjoy live music, Community stalls, arts & crafts and children's entertainment.

12 The River Thames to Woolwich Reach

The Thames Estuary is an utterly vast expanse of water accentuated by shallows and channels. The Yantlet Channel is marked by centre line buoys to provide large vessels with a deep-water channel called Black Deep, Fisherman's Gat and Princes; shipping channels which are named: Sea Reach near Southend, The Lower Hope, Gravesend Reach, Northfleet Hope, St Clement's or Fiddler's Reach, Long Reach, Erith Reach and Erith Rand, Halfway Reach, Barking Reach, Gallions Reach, Woolwich Reach by the Thames Barrier.

In 1929 the MP John Burns once famously described the river as "liquid history" – the actual quote was "The St Lawrence is water, the Mississippi is muddy water, but the Thames is liquid history". With a total length of 380 kilometres, the River Thames flows through southern England. It is the longest river entirely in England and the second longest in the United Kingdom, after the River Severn.

The river gives its name to three informal areas: The Thames Valley, Thames Gateway; and the greatly overlapping Thames Estuary around the tidal Thames to the east of London and including the waterway itself. Thames Valley Police is a formal body that takes its name from the river.

With its waters varying from freshwater to pure seawater, the Thames supports a variety of wildlife and has a number of adjoining sites of special scientific Interest. The population of grey and harbour seals numbers up to 700 in the Thames Estuary. Bottle nose dolphins and harbour porpoises are also often sighted in the Thames

Hadleigh Castle

The romantic ruins which was once a royal castle overlooks the Essex marshes and Thames Estuary. Hadleigh Castle was begun in about 1230 by Hubert de Burgh, but extensively refortified as a royal residence in 1360-70 by Edward III. The barbican and the two striking eastern drum towers added later were once seemingly used by Georgian revenue force looking out for smugglers.

Get your walking boots on and walk from the castle to Leigh on Sea or Southend. The castle is ruinous but it still has great prominence looking out over the Thames estuary. Most of it fell down hundreds of years ago while stone was salvaged by locals to build their homes.

The English painter John Constable visited Hadleigh in 1814 and made a drawing of the castle as preparation for ten oil sketches and a single painting. The painting now hangs in the Yale Center for British Art at New Haven, United States.

Canvey Island

Canvey Island is reclaimed land in the Thames estuary, it was drained and embanked by the Dutch engineer Cornelius Vermuyden in the 17th century. It is separated from the mainland of south Essex by a network of creeks. The Dutch workers and their families settled here and they built unusual octagonal cottages of which two still remain. The one in Haven Road, was built in 1621 and is still in private ownership. It has been restored and redecorated by a private owner.

Dutch Cottage

The second cottage is on Canvey Road and was built in 1618 and is now run by the Borough Council's behalf, by the Benfleet and District Historical Society as the Dutch Cottage Museum. Acquired by the council in 1952 it was restored, repainted and had its conical roof re-thatched and opened as a museum in 1962. The rooms of the cottage, which include a living room, passage and large and small bedrooms, now incorporate a variety of exhibits that illustrate the history of Canvey Island.

Canvey Island lying only just above sea level is in danger by Spring and Autumn tides of flooding at exceptional high tides. The North Sea flood of 1953 devastated the island; costing the lives of 58 islanders, but has always been inhabited since the Roman invasion of Britain.

Canvey popularized for residential homes when bought by Frederick Hester at the end of the 19th century. He advertised seaside plots to Londoners, calling Canvey an extra 'lung' for London, and out they came. Thousands of people from London flocked there. The sea front was developed in the 1930s with amusements, a cinema and the Art Deco Labworth Cafe plus all the usual beach amusements.

The island was the site of the first delivery in the world of liquefied natural gas by container ship, and later became the subject of an influential assessment on the risks to a population living within the vicinity of petrochemical shipping and storage facilities.

The Labworth Café - Digital Art

This pioneering modernist Art Deco style reinforced concrete building overlooking the Thames estuary at Labworth beach on Canvey Island. Built in 1932–1933 by Ove Arup to resemble the bridge of the Queen Mary, it is the only building designed entirely by this eminent engineer.

The Canvey Island Monsters

Two strange corpses were washed up on the south shore near Dead Mans Bay on Canvey, one in November 1953. A second, more intact, carcass was discovered in August 1954.

Not exactly fashion — and certainly not a gift, except perhaps to an angler. Pictured on Canvey Beach. What is it?

This monster fish with feet, taken by Rev. Joseph Overs

It was described as being 73 centimeters in length, and having 'thick reddish-brown skin and bulging eyes, and gills.' It was also said as having 'hind legs with five-toed horseshoe shaped feet with concave arches, but no forelimbs.' It's remains were soon cremated out of fear of the unknown.

Resident Colin Day describes coming across the carcass as a boy:" I was THERE. I was a young lad of nine at the time. I noticed a group of peers in a crowd on the beach. Kids were prodding it with their spades. I ACTUALLY TOUCHED IT! I thought it was a person at first as I could only see part of it through the crowd. Its flesh was NOT fish-like scales. It was a pinkish colour and looked like wobbly human flesh with cellulite (orange peel texture). I remember shouting to the other kids. "It's a mermaid" over and over. I have to say that even at 66, my long term memory is excellent, especially about the day I saw my first mermaid."

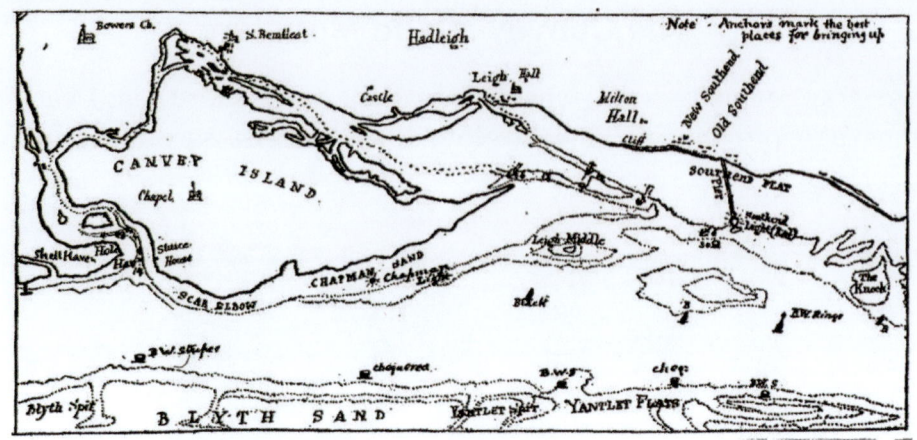

Map of the River Thames, Essex at Canvey Island, 1895

The Concrete barge was Canvey's icon, until 2003, when it was smashed up and sunk. Once destined to be a sailing club house, the local council demanded it be sunk for safety reasons after a storm swept it around from its anchorage.

Someone has christened the barge Kitty. There's a crayon cross marking its weathered hulk and an inscription: 'In Memory of the crew of the Heavenly Body II, killed near here. 379 BG, 19-6-1944.' The message and its meaning referring to the B17 of 379 Bomber Group an American Flying Fortress, one of two that collided in mid-air over the Thames on 19th June 1944 with fatal consequences. Two Tree Island next to Canvey was reclaimed from the sea in the 1700s for rough grazing and originally called Oxfleet at the Southend to East side and Haughness at the Hadleigh West side named after the two great elms brought down by a storm in 1962s.

The Concrete barge

Chapman Lighthouse-Low Tide

The Chapman light was demolished about 1957, after serving for a period of about 100 years as a Thamesmouth Pilotage and navigational aid to shipping. It was sited just over half a mile from the Canvey foreshore. Summer morning - low water on the Chapman sands - Sea reach.

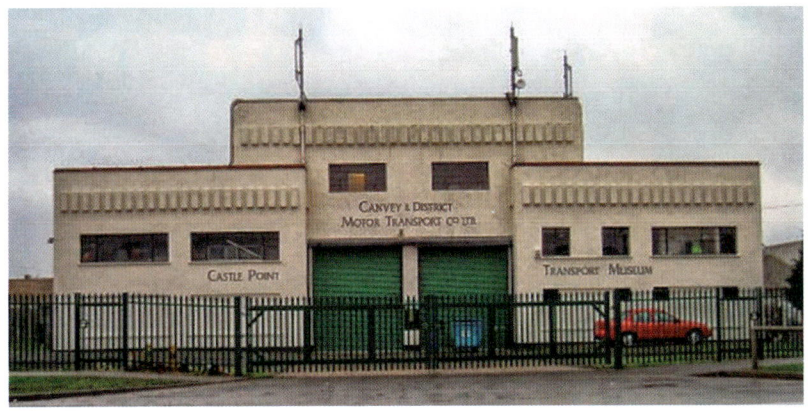

Canvey's Castle Point Transport Museum

You are welcome to visit us on the First and Third Sundays of each month between April and October, and every Sunday in the month of August.

There is no charge for entry, though donations are very welcome! Museum volunteers will be on hand to show you round and answer your questions. Our Museum shop will also be open.

Tilbury Town, Port and Fort

Before the arrival of the railway at Tilbury in 1854, there were just a few locals living in the area. Following the arrival of the railway many railway workers settled in the area. Originally called Tilbury Fort, but was later shortened to Tilbury. In 1936 the name was changed again to Tilbury Riverside: by 1992 the station was closed. Although the railway tracks have gone, the very intriguing booking hall remains. With the building of the docks which was completed in 1886, today's modern town was born.

Tilbury was a major target for German bombing during the second World War. Many houses were lost, including the Tilbury Hotel and railway station which were hit by V2 rockets.

The Draw Bridge at Tilbury Fort (often used in films)

The 1953 a great tidal surge resulted in massive flooding. 2,500 homes in Tilbury were flooded, and 1,300 people were evacuated. This event took place all the way along the Essex coast with a devastating loss of life and property.

The Port of Tilbury lies on the Essex shore of the River Thames, 40 kilometres from London Bridge. The Docks Construction begins on 17th July 1882 and the finished deep water docks were open on 17th April 1886. The vessel 'Glenfruin' made the inaugural entry. Goods, including madeira brought in by the West Africa Line; casks of sausage skins packed in brine and Indian chutney.

Tilbury Power Station Radar Tower

London Gateway is a development on the north bank of the River Thames near Thurrock, Essex, 32 kilometres east of central London. It is located on the former 1,500 acre Shell Haven site, which closed in 1999. It comprises a new deep-water port, which is able to handle the biggest container ships in the world. The port includes a 2.7 kilometres long container quay, with a capacity of 3.5 million TEU unit a year when fully developed, and is being developed in phases. The port is located on the Thames and is the nearest to London. At present it is operating way below capacity.

Etchings of Tilbury Fort Essex

During the 20th century, Tilbury Docks was a main port for the grain trade. The grain terminal, which opened in 1969, with 2000 tons per hour being unloaded. The grain silo had a 100,000-ton capacity with nearby mills ready to turn the grain to flour.

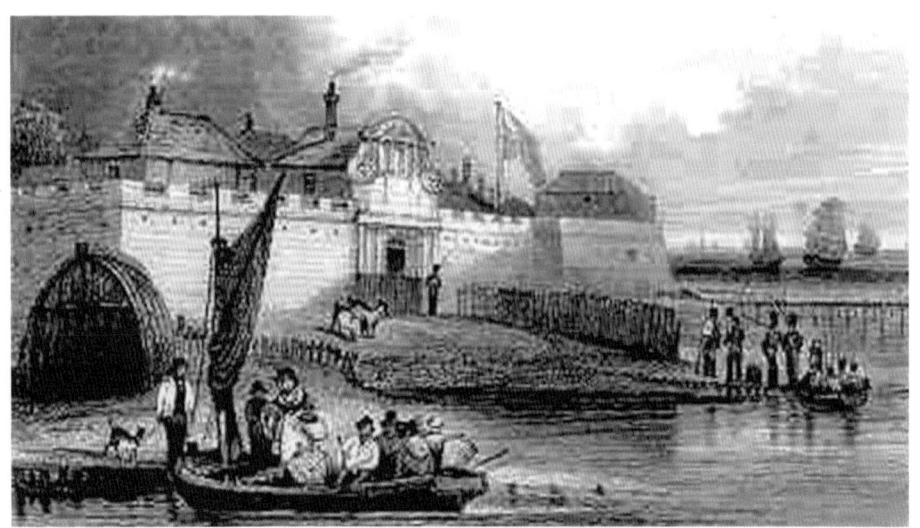

Tilbury Fort Engraving

Grays

Grays is the largest town in the Thurrock area. Towards London from Tilbury on the Thames estuary on the northern side of the river just 2 miles from the Dartford Tunnel and Bridge (a visible land mark from many miles). Its name derives from a medieval Knight from Norman times called "Anchetil De Greye" who's descendent son "Henri de Grai" acts and service were rewarded by being given these lands by King Richard 1st back in 1195. Samuel Pepys famously recorded in his diary that he visited Grays on 24 September 1665 and apparently bought fish from the local fishermen.

Grays Beach is the site of the local landmark The Gull, a lightship built in 1860. The former light vessel LV38 is rapidly deteriorating on Gray's beach. At least two fires have been lit by vandals on board and the bow has been to a great extent damaged by fire that an iron hawse hole has burned out of the structure and is now lying on the beach.

The Gull Lightship Digital Art

Grays was formerly a small port, with chalk quarries, brickworks, and a brewery.

Ford Dagenham, Essex

Over 80 years of production at Ford Dagenham

In the year 2011 Ford of Britain celebrated its centenary 80 years of production at Ford Dagenham, it's the largest UK facility on the banks of the River Thames.

From Edsel Ford digging the first turf in May 1929 to the first vehicle, a Model AA truck, rolling off the production line on 1 October 1931, Ford's Dagenham estate took 28 months to build. Move forward 80 years and Dagenham remains Ford's largest UK facility and one of the country's major automotive centres.

Dagenham today is home to an engine plant, a stamping plant and tool room, a power-train engineering team and a substantial transport operation. Some 4,500 people work on the Dagenham Estate. In 80 plus years, nearly 11 million vehicles and more than 38 million engines have rolled off the production line at the 475-acre site, much of the deliveries and exports being conveyed by the River Thames.

Did you know? Eurovision song contest winner Sandy Shaw was a punch-card operator at Dagenham before she took off her shoes to sing. Sir Malcolm Campbell land speed record-breaker was a director of Ford. Although an urban industrial site, Dagenham has its varied range of wildlife with over 50 different species of bird life making Fords land their home.

The River Thames Flood Barrier

The barrier was completed in 1982 and took 10 years to build, the Thames Barrier is one of the largest movable flood barriers in the world after the Oosterscheldekering in the Netherlands. The Barrier spans 520 metres across the River Thames near Woolwich Reach; it protects 125 square kilometres of central London from flooding caused by tidal surges. It became operational in 1982 and has 10 steel gates that can be raised into position across the River Thames. When raised, the main gates stand as high as a 5-storey building and as wide as the opening of Tower Bridge. Each main gate weighs 3,300 tonnes.

A Thames Barrier flood defence closure is triggered when a combination of high tides forecast in the North Sea and high river flows at the tidal limit at Teddington weir indicate that water levels would exceed 4.87 metres in central London.

As well as the Thames Barrier, the smaller gates along the Thames tideway include Barking Barrier, King George V lock gate, Dartford Barrier and gates at Tilbury Docks and Canvey Island must also be closed.

Barking Creek Barrier

12 The Essex Coastal History

Back in the early 20th century a vast fleet of 6,000 steamers and 5,000 sailing vessels make their way up The River Thames passing Southend on way, with an aggregate of 6,000,000 tons burden. To understand clearly what life, and excitement, and perpetual going and coming this entails, there could be no more stirring or instructive sight than the Victoria and Albert Docks. Some of the great steamers are like floating streets, almost as populous, with rooms like palaces, and decks as clean as village hearthstones. From gigantic port-holes strange wild faces and turbaned heads look out; the quays swarm with oriental workers in blue and white tunics, with Africans in cast-off garments from Wapping, with Chinamen in curious pointed shoes, and pigtails neatly tied up for convenience.

Above decks the officers may be heard giving their orders in Hindostanee; the red-turbaned sailors speak to their mates in unknown tongues; the howl with which a rope is hauled in or a bale is lowered is not unlike the cry of tigers in the jungle.

London Dockland 1950's

A maritime county of Essex, bounded on the North by Suffolk, on the East by the North Sea, on the South by Kent, on the West by Cambridge, its boundary line along a great part of the North is the river Stour, along all the South is the River Thames, along much of the West is the Rivers Lea and Stort. Its outline is irregularly four-sided, the longest line along the North, the shortest along the South.

Its greatest length from north-east to south-west is about 63 miles, its breadth from North to South is 50 miles, its circuit is about 225 miles, and its area is 987,028 acres, making it the tenth English county for size. Its coast is so irregular and broken that the exact length of it cannot easily be ascertained, but including much on the River Thames, and not reckoning estuaries. Its chief headlands are the Naze, over five miles South of Harwich, Foulness at the mouth of the Crouch river, and Shoeburyness at the mouth of the Thames. Shoals of sands lie off some parts, and numerous islands, situated within the general coast-line, and divided by only narrow belts of water from the interior tracts, diversify others. The chief islands are Horsey near the Naze, Mersea at the mouth of Blackwater river, Wallasea and Foulness at the mouth of the Crouch River, and Canvey on the Thames.

The seaboard is low, flat, and partly marshy, has suffered much devastation and fracture by encroachments of the sea, and except to a smaller extent at Harwich, Southend, and Purfleet, is protected from further injury by strong embankments. The highest grounds are Langdon Hill and Danebury Camp, and these have an altitude of about 620 feet. Much of the surface, from combination of natural feature and artificial embellishment, exhibits a pleasing and ever-varying succession of rural landscapes. The chief rivers, besides those which run on the boundaries, are the Colne, the Blackwater, the Chelmer, the Crouch, the Roding, the Ingerburn, the Wid, and the Brain. The geognostic formation of much of the seaboard is fresh water deposit, of most of the rest of the county is London clay, and of the tract around Castle Hedingham and Thaxted, and that to the northern and western boundaries, is chalk.

The soil throughout the county is rather various; on the seaboard both of the ocean and of the Thames is generally marshy with inter mixture of gravel, in the district of the Rodings is strong wet loam, in the central and northern parts is variously strong and moist, light and loamy, in the western parts varies from tough clay upon brick earth to thin loam upon gravel, and in many places is either good meadow, light gravel, or rich loam. Much improvement has been done by draining, top-dressing, and other geological practices. Extracts from The Comprehensive Gazetteer of England and Wales, 1894-5

Map of the Essex Boundary 1885

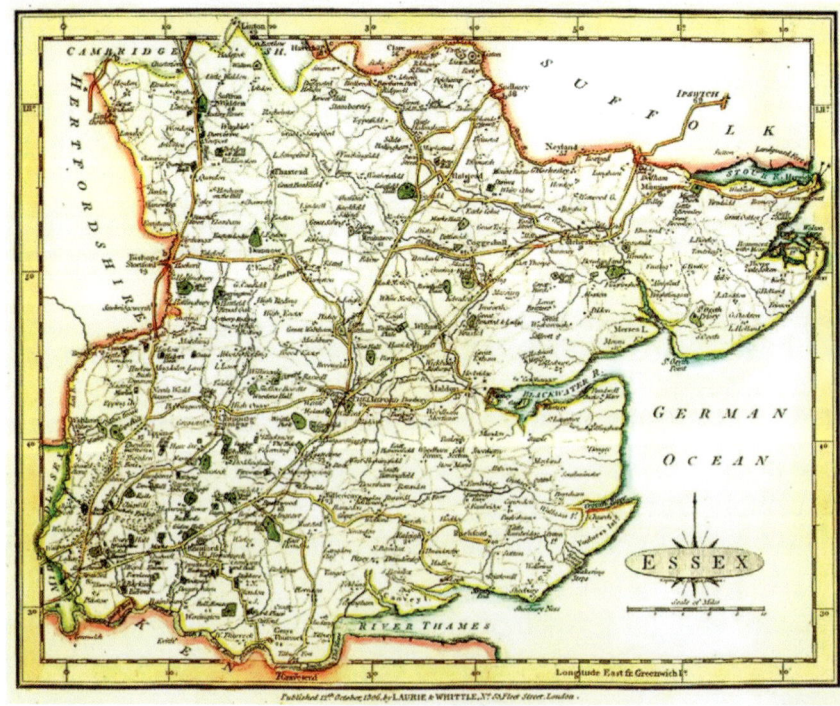

Jonathan Potter Map of Essex 1806 (North Sea was Called German Ocean)

Essex lifeboat Stations

Royal National Lifeboat Institution (RNLI) stations are the bases for the RNLI's fleet of search and rescue lifeboats that cover the coastal waters around the entire British Isles, as well as major inland waterways. The service was established in 1824 and is operated largely by volunteers. Its headquarters are at Poole in Dorset. It is registered as a charity in both the United Kingdom and Republic of Ireland.

Essex based lifeboat stations are at:

1. Harwich Lifeboat station is one of the busiest in Britain and is just one of the 230 RNLI stations based about the Britain coast. Today there are two lifeboats stationed at Harwich the off-shore Severn class lifeboat "Albert Brown" and the inshore Atlantic 75 lifeboat "Sure and Steadfast".

2. Walton and Frinton has celebrated over 120 years as a lifeboat station and its crews have been presented with 75 awards for gallantry. The lifeboat was one of 19 lifeboats that helped to evacuate the British Expeditionary Force from Dunkirk.

3. Clacton on Sea Lifeboat Station saving lives at sea since 1878. They operate an Atlantic 85 class lifeboat; gift shop opening times 11am until 3pm seven Days a Week

4. Burnham-on-Crouch RNLI operates a Atlantic 75 and a IB1 Lifeboat from the Lifeboat station on the River Crouch at Burnham yacht Harbour at Foundry Lane, Burnham on Crouch, Essex, CM0 8BL

5. Southend-on-Sea lifeboat station has a remarkable history of bravery with 59 awards for gallantry. It is the only station to operate three inshore lifeboats. The busiest lifeboat stations in the country, averaging over 100 'shouts' per year.

The RNLI is the charity that saves lives at sea

Donate by post send a cheque, payable to

Royal National Lifeboat Institution, West Quay Road, Poole, BH15 1HZ

Donate by phone UK: 0300 300 9990 Monday-Friday 8am-6pm

or on the net at **https://rnli.org/donateorbecomeamember**

Walton & Frinton RNLI Lifeboat at the pier

Southend lifeboat station

James Stevens No 14 Harwich lifeboat

Essex Coastguard

A Coastguard service has played an important part in the life of coastal Essex since customs men were first introduced in the 12th century. They are also of strong genealogical interest given the employment rule that ensured that recruits were posted to areas where they had no family. This was required to prevent collaboration between smugglers and Coastguard's. Essex was a hotbed of smuggling and as such had one of the highest populations of Coastguard's in the country living on watch vessels usually old vessels, barracks or specially built watchtower houses.

Bradwell Waterside in 1857 showing customs coastguard gunboat

The Coastguard remained under the control of the Board of Trade until the outbreak of the Second World War, when it passed in succession to the Ministry of Shipping (1939-40); Admiralty (1940-45); and Ministry of War Transport (1945- 1964). It then returned to the Department of Trade until 1983 when responsibility passed to the Department of Transport. The service became a government executive agency in the 1990s and is currently run by the Maritime and Coastguard Agency.

In the 1960s a programme of modernization was initiated in response to the post-war popularity of leisure craft and small boats, which had led to a significant increase in seaside incidents. As a result, there was a shift in emphasis to co-ordination of search and rescue operations, facilitated by improvements in communication technology. This led to a move away from the coastal watch in Coastguard stations to the remote monitoring of ship movements from Maritime Rescue Co-ordination Centre.

By 1903 the number of stations had reached 533, when the Admiralty decided to acquire all leased property and, where necessary, build new premises, at an estimated cost of £200,000. Just a few years later the Admiralty began closing stations and 79 were shut between 1907 and 1912.

Rescues from stricken vessels have taken place on the Essex cost ever since man began to use boats. Co-ordination of rescues would be the responsibility of ships captains or in the case of a boat running aground the local JP or Squire. Appointing a body to be responsible for rescue from wrecks only took place in 1809.

Smugglers from the continent were a problem from the 1600's and as a result the Board of Customs appointed customs officers in ports and fitted out Revenue ships to patrol the channel coast and deter smuggling. By 1700 a formal force, called Riding Officers. These Officers were to patrol the coast to catch the smugglers in the act of landing if they managed to avoid the Revenue Ships and Customs Officers in ports. The Board of Excise appointed its own Revenue Ships and Riding Officers to cover Essex.

In 1809 two more forces were added with formation of the Water Guard to patrol coastal waters in small boats and the Coast blockade to assist the riding officers. The Water guard effectively was the forerunner of our modern coastguard by being given responsibility for saving lives in wrecks.

Essex proved attractive to smugglers given the many creeks and inlets used by the Thames barges and the marshy nature of the coast prevented riding officer's patrols and made concealment difficult for groups of revenue men. To help combat this Watch Vessels were introduced in greater number than anywhere else in the country effectively blocking the major routes in the Rivers.

By 1923 a more complex marine safety agency was required and the water based revenue collection needs had changed which meant that the responsibility for revenue was given to the new HM Customs and Excise Department and the Coastguard was given the responsibility for life saving rescue from wrecks and administration of the foreshore.

In 1830 the Coastguard was formed by a merger of the Water Guard with the Customs. The new body was to be controlled by the Royal Navy with the remit of preventing smuggling and dealing with shipwrecks by lifesaving and then protection from looters. This continued until 1923 when the duties were once again separated and the Coastguard was solely responsible for life saving at sea, salvage of wrecks and the administration of the rules of the sea.

By 1831 all of the forces had been amalgamated into the Coastguard. Although smugglers were the main priority the responsibility of saving victims of wreck remained. In 1856 control of the Coastguard moved from the Board of Customs to the Royal Navy and with the reduction of smuggling emphasis was more focused on saving lives at sea.

Her Majesty's Watch Vessel Kangeroo

The Admiralty used hulks and beached ships as accommodation for Coastguards, particularly in Essex.

The Essex Martello Towers

Originally 103 towers were built between 1805 and 1812. A line of defensive fortresses to defend the coastal towns from Napoleon's forces. 29 towers were built between Aldeburgh and St Osyth's between 1808 and 1812 to protect Essex and Suffolk, the rest having been built a few years earlier across the Kent and Sussex coasts. They were built of brick, 13-foot-thick on the seaward side, stood about 30-foot-high and were armed with a cannon on the roof. It is estimated that one million bricks were used in the construction of each tower. The towers were designated with a letter of the alphabet A to K, five are no longer around G, H, I, J, plus tower Martello B was converted to a home then demolished in 1967

Martello A from Brightlingsea

Martello A at Point Clear Bay contains the East Essex Aviation Society and Museum

Martello C at Jaywick used by Essex County Council as an arts venue for visual and digital arts. On the roof, is a purpose-built look-out station.

Martello D on the walk from Clacton-on-Sea to Jaywick, unused

Martello E located at Clacton - once a water tower, now unused

Martello F at Clacton now partly sunk into the earth bank was once a model village within a moat, a watch station on the top, a restaurant now a Children's Zoo

Martello K at Walton Private, unused

St Osyth was the location for Martello Tower 'B' on Beacon Heights. This tower was demolished in the middle 1970's. Owned by Mr Hyde who was a keen amateur astronomer, he became a pioneer in Radio Astronomy with the tower roof housing a number of radio detection aerials to pick up signals from space. He was one of the first to pick up the signal from the Russian Sputnik the first Earth-orbiting artificial satellite launched on 4 October 1957. Following this success, he formed a minor partner collaboration with Sir Bernard Lovell who was in charge of the world first steerable dish radio telescope (now known as the Lovell telescope), which was 250 ft in diameter, when it was completed in 1957.

The name Martello is derived from Torre della Mortella, a circular fortress in Corsica which held out to British attack for a few days until it was eventually captured. The attackers were so impressed by its defensive capabilities, that its plan was adopted and modified to suit our coast. A supporting fort named Redoubt, was built at Harwich. By 1812 the towers were completed and ready for battle, but none of the towers were ever used in anger against the French or any other country.

Martello Tower F at Clacton, a watch station, a restaurant, it's even had a model railway but now a Children's Zoo

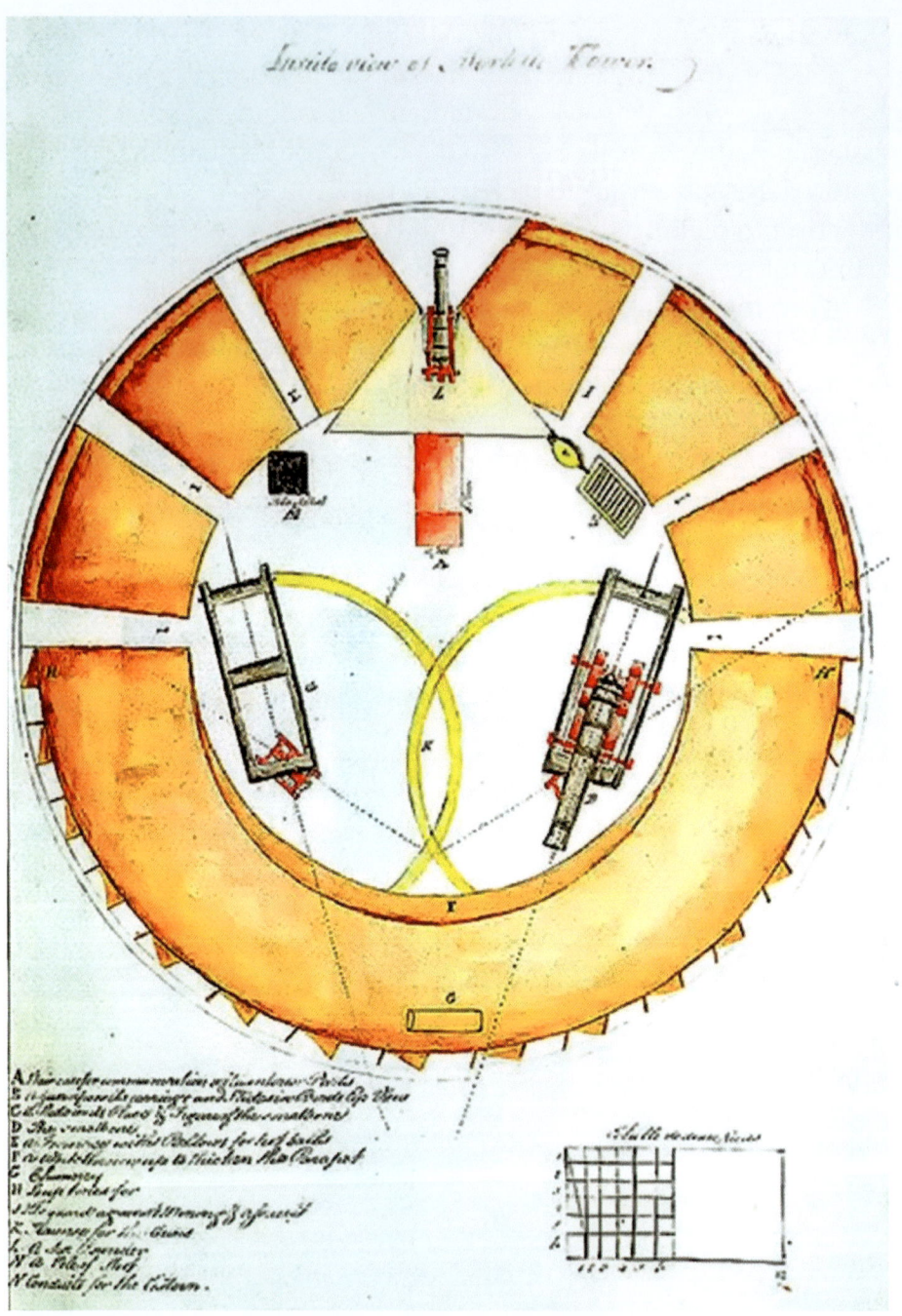

Plan of Tour de Mortella c.1794, Corsica the inspiration for the English Marello Tower

Essex Bird and Wildlife Groups

- **East London Birders' Forum**
- **Essex Field Club**
- **Essex Wildlife Trust**
- **Friends of Heybridge Gravel Pits**
- **Holland Haven Birding**
- **North Thames Gull Group**
- **Southend Ornithological Group**
- **South East Essex RSPB Group**
- **South Essex Natural History Society**

Essex Nature Reserves

- **Old Hall Marshes RSPB Nature Reserve**
- **Paxton Pits NR**
- **Rainham Marshes RSPB Nature Reserve**
- **South Essex Marshes RSPB Nature Reserve**
- **Stour Estuary RSPB Nature Reserve**
- **Vange Marsh RSPB Nature Reserve**
- **Wallasea Island Wild Coast project**
- **West Canvey Marsh RSPB Nature Reserve**

Stanford Warren Nature Reserve

This 41 acre Thames-side reserve consists of one of the largest reedbeds in Essex, created by gravel extraction in the 1920s, together with areas of marsh and rough grassland.

Chafford Gorges Nature Park

This visitor centre is set in a spectacular position over looking Warren Gorge. This nature park offers 200 acres of green space for numerous wildlife and recreation for the 12,500 people living in Chafford Hundred.

Fobbing Marsh Nature Reserve

This 187 acre site is one of the few remaining Thameside grazing marshes, part of which was fortified in the aftermath of the 1953 floods.

Two Tree Island Nature Reserve

This 640 acre island is situated south of Leigh on Sea train station. The island itself consists of grassland, scrub, reedbed and lagoons and supports a wide variety of birds, particularly migrants. Avocets breed on the island each year.

Gunners Park and Shoebury Ranges Nature Reserve

This nature reserve incorporates the Shoebury Old Ranges Site of Special Scientific Interest (SSSI) and the Coastguard Station Grounds Local Wildlife Site, totaling 25 hectares.

Ray Island and Bonners Saltings Nature Reserve

This 100 acre reserve comprises Ray Island which is a large sandy mound rising out of the surrounding saltings. Access by boat only.

Colne Point Nature Reserve

This large and important 683 acre reserve at the mouth of the Colne Estuary and consists of a shingle ridge enclosing a considerable area of saltmarsh, through which Ray Creek flows. It is an important nesting site for Little Terns.

Howlands Marsh Nature Reserve

This 74 acre reserve is one of the best surviving coastal grazing marshes in Essex, consisting mainly of low lying hummocky grassland, split up by dykes and fleets.

Cockaynes Wood Nature Reserve

Cockaynes Wood is ancient Essex woodland, listed in the Domesday Book of 1086. The 50-acre 'Cockaynes Wood nature reserve' also includes a former quarry, dry heath, grassy meadows and shallow water ponds.

Great Holland Pits Nature Reserve

A former gravel pit, this 40 acre reserve includes heathy grassland, pasture, a remnant of old woodland, large and small pools and wet depressions. There are attractive views of Holland Brook meandering through water meadows.

Skipper's Island Nature Reserve

This 233 acre reserve is surrounded by saltmarsh. The island has large stands of Sea Hog's-fennel, food plant of Fisher's Estuarine Moth. There is no access to the island.

Copperas Wood Nature Reserve

This 34 acre ancient wood consists mainly of coppiced sweet Chestnut and Hornbeam. It was severely damaged in the great storm of 1987 and sections of the wood have been left in their devastated state for wildlife value and for scientific study.

Essex Way: Wrabness to Manningtree

Wrabness Nature Reserve

This 60 acre reserve offers fantastic views on the southern bank of the Stour Estuary. Grassland, scrub and woodland offer a variety of habitats. As does the wonderful adjoining marsh.

Essex Wildlife

Walk the Essex coast and find a magnificence of wildlife and stories on the way. Up and down the numerous creeks and estuaries of this the longest county shoreline of any English coastal county. Essex Wildlife Trust is the county's leading conservation charity. It has more than 33,000 members, manages and protects over 7,250 acres of land on 87 nature reserves and 2 nature parks and runs 9 visitor centres. The aim of Essex Wildlife Trust is to Protect Wildlife for the Future.

Essex nature reserves like Fingringhoe are especially renowned for sea birds like the avocet, a fleeting glance of a Kingfisher or an oystercatcher which are beautifully eye-catching when they take off in flocks, be lucky and sight the rarer marsh harrier. Birds are beautiful to behold and listen to, and their variety is almost endless in size and shape. Wild birds are also a window into the health and changes of a better or worse environment.

Avocet Wading Birds, Digital Art

At this reserve you may spot Nightingale, Cliff Chaff, Whitethroat, Cuckoo, Thyme-leaved Speedwell, Foxglove, Common Vetch, Orange Tip Butterfly and Speckled Wood. In the early summer Marsh Harrier, Great crested Grebe, Turtle Dove, Sand Martin, Swallow, Hobby, Common Spotted Orchid, Green Alkanet, Common Lizard and Slow Worm.

Fingringhoe Wick was Essex Wildlife Trust's first nature reserve opened in 1961 and some years later it was where the Trust opened their first visitor centre, and fifty years on visitors are still coming to see this magical place. Set in a spectacular position overlooking the Colne Estuary the visitor centre provides stunning views over the estuary. The visitor centre facilities include gift shop, viewing tower and observation room with panoramic views, toilets, baby changing facilities, wheel chair and there is a hearing loop available.

The outstanding position of the centre overlooking the Colne Estuary so even on the dullest of days the views and sightings can be splendid. It offers the visitor real peace and quiet and a chance to escape from it all. A broad range of habitats are here to be viewed, including grassland, heathland and ponds some can be seen from a couple of fittingly well located viewing hides from which you may see: a flock if Canada Geese, or perhaps twenty or maybe Oyster Catchers glistering in the sunlight as they twist and turn in flight, there is often bullfinch or chaffinch eating from the feeder outside the centre.

Fingringhoe Wick Nature Reserve and Visitor Centre

Address: South Green Road, Fingringhoe, Colchester, Essex, CO5 7DN
Phone: 01206 729678 Email: **fingringhoe@essexwt.org.uk**
Opening hours: Tuesday – Sunday 9am – 5pm, Bank holidays 9am – 5pm (Closed Christmas Day and Boxing Day)

Other Essex Coast reserves:

Thurrock Thameside Nature Park

Cory Environmental Trust Visitor Centre, Mucking Wharf Road, Mucking, Stanford-le-Hope, Essex, SS17 0RN

Tel: 01375 643342 Email: **ttnp@essexwt.org.uk**

Opening hours: Tuesday to Sunday 9am – 5pm

The Thurrock Thameside Nature Park at Mucking Flats and the Thames Estuary, which lies on top of 50 years of waste from six London boroughs, has been restored to grasslands, woodland, ponds and reedbeds. Footpaths and cycleways in 120 acres of nature park. Spendid birdwatching - and passing ship watching. Facilities: Shop selling toys and gifts, Starling's Tearooms selling drinks and hot food, Learning Zone, seating area, toilets, panoramic roof top viewing platform with free to view telescope. Essex Wildlife Trust is working to transform Mucking landfill site into a Living Landscape, this is the biggest project Essex Wildlife Trust has ever undertaken.

Belfairs Woodland Centre

Eastwood Road North, Leigh on Sea, Essex, SS9 4LR

Tel: 01702 477467 Email: **belfairs@essexwt.org.uk**

Opening hours: Every day 10am – 4pm

Belfairs Woodland Centre is open daily, 9am - 5pm. The Woodland Centre provides a space for schools, groups and families to learn about south Essex's ancient woodlands.

West Canvey Marsh

Open at all times with car park open daily from 9 am to 5 pm.

This Nature reserve is the largest single area of green space on Canvey Island. This wonderful wetland includes nearly two miles (3 km) of new nature trails, three viewing points, a picnic area and children's adventure area. The 256 hectares of saltmarsh and grassland will now form part of a huge network of special places for wildlife straddling the Thames in Essex. This is a great place to start looking for birds, especially in winter when there are plenty of waders and the chance to see a short-eared owl.

Tel: 01268 498620 e-mail: **southessex@rspb.org.uk**

Rainham Marshes Nature Reserve

RSPB Rainham Marshes Nature Reserve The Visitor Centre, New Tank Hill Road, Purfleet, Essex, RM19 1SZ
Tel: 01708 899840
E-mail: **rainham.marshes@rspb.org.uk**
http://www.rspb.org.uk/discoverandenjoynature/seenature/reserves/guide/r/rainhammarshes/about.aspx
Rainham Marshes is an RSPB nature reserve to the east of London, adjacent to the Thames Estuary in Purfleet, Thurrock and the London Borough of Havering. In 2000, the area of land was bought from the Ministry of Defence, who used it as a test firing range. With no activity for several years, the nature reserve was officially opened to the public in 2006. It has maintained much of its Medieval landscape, and is the largest area of wetland on the upper parts of the Thames Estuary. One of very few ancient landscapes remaining in London, these medieval marshes right next to the River Thames are a unique nature reserve, restored to a grazing marshland after 100 years of use as a MoD shooting range.

Useful Essex Coastal Addresses and Websites:

Essex Birdwatching Society are the county bird society for Essex and collate data on the status of birds within Essex. http://www.ebws.org.uk/ebs/default.asp

Fingringhoe Wick Visitor Centre: South Green Road, Fingringhoe, Colchester, CO5 7DN

Nature reserve 125 acres of mixed habitat on the Colne Estuary. Nature trails, wheelchair access, bird hides.

Northey Cottage, Northey Island, Maldon.

Small Island in the Blackwater Estuary, undisturbed salt marsh. Site of special scientific interest & the Battle of the Maldon in AD991.

RSPB Bobbit's Hole Nature Reserve Main Rd, Dovercourt, CO12 3HJ

A small nature reserve of approx 2 acres with a small pond.

Tollesbury Wick Marshes near: Maldon.

Essex Wildlife Trust's best reserves. A large tract of ancient grazing marsh that is managed as a traditional coastal farm.

RSPB Old Hall Marshes Nature Reserve 1 Old Hall Lane, Tolleshunt D'Arcy, CM9 8TP

An opportunity to see an abundance of coastal wetland bird species in their natural environment.

RSPB Stour Estuary Nature Reserve Harwich Road, Wrabness, CO12 5ND

Estuarine nature reserve, with adjacent woodland & views over the Stour.

RSPB Wallasea Island Creeksea Ferry Road, Essex, SS4 2HD

http://www.rspb.org.uk/discoverandenjoynature/seenature/reserves/guide/w/wallaseaisland/ A landmark conservation and engineering scheme for the 21st century.

RSPB West Canvey Marsh Canvey Island, SS8 0PS

Wetland reserve nature trails, three viewing points, a picnic area and children's adventure area.

The Naze is located just north of Walton-on-the-Naze, in North East Essex.

The beautiful Naze cliffs and national nature reserve, famous for fossils.

Bradwell Shell Bank Southminster.

Bradwell Cockle Spit on the Dengie Peninsular, 30 acres of shell bank together with saltmarsh.

Shoebury 'Old Ranges' Nature Reserve near: Southend-on-Sea

A Site of Special Scientific Interest, Shoebury's 'Old Ranges' are a fascinating habitat

Essex Horse & Pony Protection Society: Pitsea Hall Lane, Basildon, SS16 4UH

The Essex Society for Archaeology and History is the county's major society for those interested in any aspect of the past. **http://www.essex.ac.uk/history/esah/**

HM Coastguard Thames maritime rescue co-ordination centre Phone 01255 675 518

HM Coastguard, East Terrace, Walton on Naze, Essex. CO14 8PY May soon be closed.

Clacton-On-Sea Coast Guard Station, Hastings Avenue, Clacton-on-Sea, CO15 1BW

Coastguard H.M. Coastguard Station, Ness Rd, Shoeburyness, Southend-On-Sea, SS3 9QR. Tel: 01702 294998

Two Tree Island near: Leigh-on-Sea.

An outstanding 634-acre site situated off the Old Leigh coastline with a lagoon at its western tip. The island itself consists of grassland, scrub, reedbed and supports a wide variety of birds, particularly migrants like Avocets who breed on the island each year.

The Essex Way

The Essex Way guidebook is available for free download from **Essex County Council** public rights of way section. This gives points of interest & historical information about places passed along the route.

The Essex Way is a long distance footpath stretching for 82 miles right across Essex. Although it officially starts in Epping and ends in Harwich, the Essex Way actually is signposted both ways, so Essex Walkers can start at any point on the route and head either way. The route is varied and interesting, taking you through ancient woodland, open farmland, tree-lined river valleys and leafy green lanes, with plenty of picturesque and historic villages along the way.

The routes can be broken into sections so that each represented a moderately demanding walk of around 8 to 12 miles, and which could be accessed via environmentally friendly public transport. So each section of the Essex Way mentioned starts and stops either within half a mile of a train station, or near a bus stop with a regular service to a major town. There are refreshment places, referred to in the ten guides, along the route or part route you choose to take.

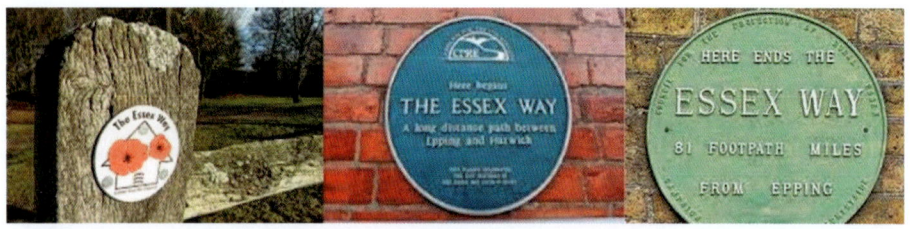

The Essex Way was conceived after a competition organised by the Campaign to Protect Rural England in 1972, and the original dark green CPRE Essex Way plaques can still be seen on some parts of the route. However, these signs have been mostly superseded by Essex County Council plaques displaying two red poppies on a white disc.

Link to Complete route in 10 stages **pdf**
http://www.essexway.org.uk/documents/exwall.pdf

Hundreds of the Essex Coast

Between Anglo-Saxon times and the nineteenth century the English county of Essex was divided for administrative purposes into 19 hundreds, plus the Liberty of Havering-atte-Bower and the boroughs of Colchester, Harwich, and Maldon. Listed here the Essex Coastal Hundreds

Dengie Hundred includes; Althorne, Asheldham, Bradwell-on-Sea, Burnham, Cold Norton, Creeksea, Dengie, Hazeleigh, Latchingdon, St Lawrence, Mayland, Mundon, North Fambridge, Purleigh, Southminster, Steeple, Stow Maries, Tillingham, Woodham Mortimer, Woodham Walter

Winstree Hundred includes; Abberton, Fingringhoe, Langenhoe, Layer Breton, Layer de la Haye, Layer Marney, East Mersea, West Mersea, Peldon, Salcott, Virley, Great Wigborough, Little Wigborough

Thurstable Hundred includes; Goldhanger, Heybridge, Langford, Tollesbury, Tolleshunt D'Arcy, Tolleshunt Knights, Tolleshunt Major, Great Totham, Little Totham, Wickham Bishops

Tendring Hundred includes; Alresford, Ardleigh, Beaumont-cum-Moze, Great Bentley, Little Bentley, Bradfield, Brightlingsea, Great Bromley, Little Bromley, Great Clacton, Little Clacton, Elmstead, Frating, Frinton, Great Holland, Little Holland, Kirby, Lawford, Manningtree, Mistley, Great Oakley, Little Oakley, St Osyth, Ramsey, Tendring, Thorpe-le-Soken, Thorrington, Walton-le-Soken, Weeley, Wix, Wrabness

Rochford Hundred includes; Ashingdon, Barling, Canewdon, Eastwood, South Fambridge, Foulness, Hadleigh, Havengore Marsh, Hawkwell, Hockley, Leigh, Paglesham, Prittlewell, Rawreth, Rayleigh, Rochford, Shopland, North Shoebury, South Shoebury, Southchurch, Great Stambridge, Little Stambridge, Sutton, Great Wakering, Little Wakering

Barstable Hundred includes; Basildon, Bowers Gifford, Bulphan, Chadwell, Corringham, Doddinghurst, Downham, Dunton, East Horndon, East Tilbury, Fobbing, Great Burstead, Horndon-on-the-Hill, Hutton, Ingrave, Laindon, Langdon Hills, Lee Chapel, Little Burstead, Little Thurrock, Mucking, Nevendon, North Benfleet, Orsett, Pitsea, Ramsden Bellhouse, Ramsden Crays, Shenfield, South Benfleet, Stanford le Hope, Thundersley, Vange, West Horndon, West Tilbury, Wickford

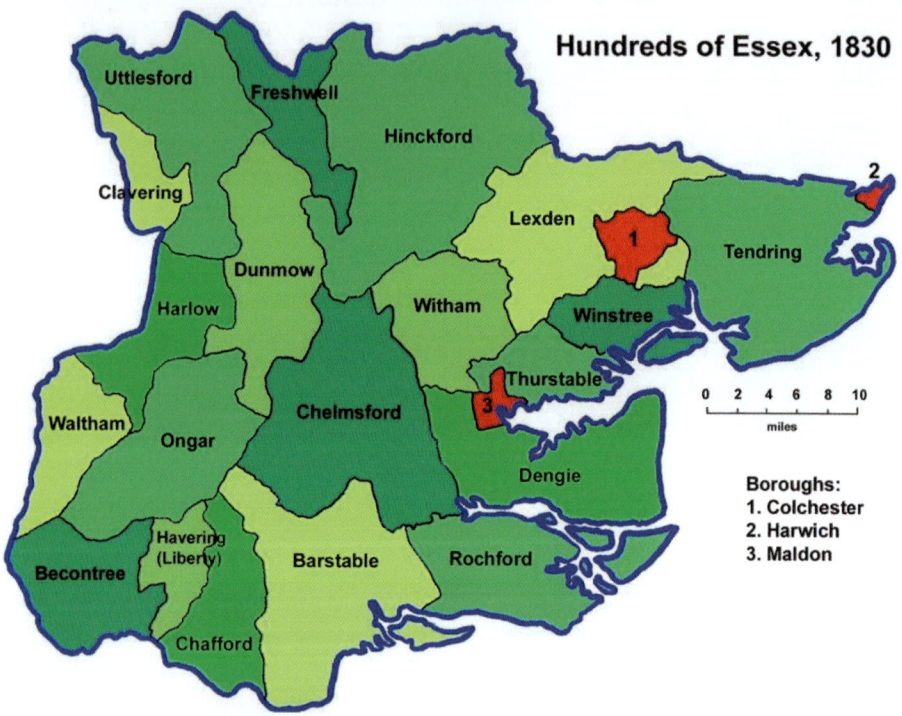

Essex Hundreds 1830

About the Author Doug Carpenter

Portrait of the author by Charles Grigg Tait

I'm sure I was born (1945) with a paint brush in my hand. I can't remember a period in my life where I wasn't drawing or painting. This lead to the inevitable comment "You'll have to be an artist when you grow up". So here I am, (I've not grown up yet though). Everyone remembers their college days with great enthusiasm. I was at Goldsmiths College in New Cross, London, which was only a cycle ride away from where I lived. I studied portrait painting and commercial art. All that back in the early 1960s. I took a job with the press in the art department, but alas we parted company, after which I was to explore my vocation as a professional artist. Starting with oil painting in the style of the old masters, to nowadays where I also embrace watercolour, digital art and photography. art-artist.co.uk

The Author Doug Carpenter at the wheel of the Thames Barge Edme

Printed in Great Britain
by Amazon